Etched Into My Soul!

BOOK
POWER
PUBLISHING

Dedicated to my parents,
Calvin and Georgia Jardan,
who instilled in us a love of education.

Words of Admiration

"In the Name of God, Most Gracious, Most Merciful"

It is with great pleasure that I share these remarks on behalf of my friend, Daaimah Jardan.

I arrived in Los Angeles, California in the summer of 1982 from Birmingham, Alabama. As a Muslim, I was anxious to find out more about the Islamic Community in Southern California. Likewise, as an educator, I was in search of employment because I had my two young children with me. It was in pursuit of these two, I met this modest, quiet, petite sister...Daaimah, whose spiritual aura was larger than any I had experienced. I found her to be a devoted Muslim and an extraordinary educator. We attended the same Mosque, as it was called then. We attended Jumu'ah together; we prayed together, and we even had exercise classes together. We both worked with the Los Angeles Unified School District until retirement.

Over the course of our tenure, we became remarkably close friends. I learned so much from her about the school district and more importantly, about Al Islam as she was born Muslim, whereas I converted after becoming an adult. I often listened and observed her because she was knowledgeable and 'spot on' when it came to various principles related to women in Islam. Daaimah is the kind of friend everyone should cherish. On numerous occasions during challenging times, she has opened her home to me and provided timely support and advice.

When I retired from the school district and moved back south, we continued to stay in touch. She was one of the first to know about and to read my book, My Life Journey: Through My Own Eyes, released in 2014. I was delighted to get her feedback. I was thrilled when she called to tell me about her book.

Congratulations my dear friend! I applaud you as you continue your journey of greatness. And thank you for being my friend. May Allah continue to Bless you in all your endeavors.

Dr. Malika Salaam-Ambolley

Daaimah Jardan. What can I say about Daaimah Jardan? I've known her for over forty years and the adventure has always been a pleasure. She is an upstanding woman, the only person I know who has been Muslim all her life - a kindhearted, giving person. A popular, well-known teacher who in her own right is always remembered by her students. We have traveled together many times and no matter where we have gone there is always a young adult walking up to her and saying "you were my teacher in X grade." She may not remember them, but her influence on them has lasted a life time.

She was my first Arabic lesson teacher, which she doesn't remember, but I do and I thank her for that experience to this very day. If anything can be said about Daaimah Jardan, it is this, she is an influencer whose presence stays with you for a lifetime. This book about her life is long overdue and eagerly awaited.

Mahasin Shamsiddeen

January 1, 2023

This letter is a testimonial to Ms. Daaimah Jardan's autobiographical book.

Ms. Daaimah Jardan has written an exciting autobiographical book about her life as a Muslim in America. It is an absorbing and educational biographical work about her life.

It covers the time from when the Honorable Elijah Muhammad was the leader of most African American Muslims in the U.S. to when Wallac D Muhammad became the leader and, most recently, a time when most mosques or masjids serving the African American Community have become independent.

Her book is an amazing story of a woman whose belief in Allah, and in her fellow African American people, allowed her to make significant contributions to her community. Currently, she is a retired Los Angeles City School Teacher during which she set high, but achievable, standards for Los Angeles City youth. As a result, she gained much community respect.

In the book she, also, describes her Hajj experience in Mecca and the impact it had on her life. It is a detailed description of what she went through and can serve as a guide to women who want to prepare for Hajj.

Ms. Jardan has met all of the key life-milestones of a sincere, believing, Muslim, and her book will serve as an important guide for future generations of Muslims.

Sincerely,
A Nelson El-Amin, MD

More than 25 years ago I first met my friend, Delores Jardan, in a computer classroom where I had just been hired to teach at a LAUSD (Los Angeles Unified School District) High School. I was a real novice when it came to computers and technology at that time since computers always scared me. But with the help that Ms. Jardan offered me I was able to learn easily. Without her being pushy or crtitical about my lack of knowledge she was able to get me to a level of understanding computers and technology where I was able to function very well at my job.

Now, my friend has written a most powerful book about family and friends which in my opinion is a masterpiece. She has the intuition, the kindness and the skills to guide you through her life in the most powerful way through her words. You will be amazed at how great this book will make you feel while reading it. I'm very proud to say that I know this author!

Yours truly,
Georgia Pettis

Etched Into My Soul!

**Expressing My Memories
and Gratitude Over Eight Decades.**

A Muslim Woman's Memoir

DELORES DAAIMAH JARDAN

BOOK
POWER
PUBLISHING

DETROIT, MICHIGAN

Contents

Publisher's Note

There was a time in American history when, by design, many people of African descent could not read or write. Their lives were seen as insignificant, and their minds deemed not worthy of accessing written knowledge. Therefore, they certainly weren't encouraged to record their own history.

It is still an absolute travesty that countless stories and untold wisdom from the African American community were lost.

Enter Black Muslims. In the 60s and 70s, African Americans came into Islam in droves. Many who were searching for a path to rectify the negative effects of the wickedness of "white supremacy," found that Islam provided a way for them to clean up their lives and their communities.

Many of those who came in during that era are now in their 70s, 80s, and 90s. They are a unique group with a unique history, much of which is at risk of being lost. It is no secret that we have a void in our collective written understanding of African Americans and certainly African American Muslims.

We can't do anything about what was lost, but we CAN do our job now to make sure that cycle ends. We understand that our history must be preserved and WE are the only ones to do it.

The journey undertaken by our beloved author, Sr. Delores Daaimah Jardan was not an easy one. She overcame obstacles that would have deterred many others. Despite the challenges, even with this book, she pressed on, her pen becoming a weapon against silence and erasure. Her determination serves as an inspiration to us all, reminding us that each of us have a life worth sharing and the lessons we've learned can help others.

In a world that often celebrates youth and novelty, it is crucial that we view this book not merely as a "story," but as a historical document. Through her words, we are invited to bear witness to a unique perspective—a testament to resilience, faith, and the triumph of the human spirit.

It is my humbling privilege to be part of the process of preserving and sharing this exceptional work. Let us be more than just "readers." We too must become the stewards of knowledge, ensuring that both our legacies, and the legacies of those who came before us endure.

Let us celebrate the achievements of Sr. Jardan, whose dedication to the written word has illuminated the path for others to follow. May her story be a beacon of hope and inspiration, reminding us all that knowledge is a timeless gift meant to be shared, cherished, and passed on for generations to come.

Zarinah El-Amin
Founder, Book Power Publishing

Author's Note

A lot of people know that I was born and raised in the Nation of Islam. They ask me about my life, and they ask me about my parents. This book is my answer.

As of today, I am 87 years old. I have been blessed to see many things in my life. Many ups and downs. Many of the historical moments they talk about, I lived through and witnessed first-hand.

I authored this book to capture my thoughts and experiences over my 87 years. You will learn about my family and my friends. Additionally, you will learn about the historical figures of Islam I met in my life, and the trials brought on by others.

A big part of my book is showing gratitude to the many people who have influenced, assisted, guided, and aided me throughout my life. This list is not exclusive, and I do not intentionally exclude anyone. I have tried to mention as many people as I could who have played a positive role in my life.

I hope this book will increase the reader's knowledge of Al Islam and answer any questions he or she wants to know but never had the opportunity to ask.

Additionally, I would like for my daughter, grandchildren, and other younger family members, and people in general, to search their family history. It is educational and interesting.

Delores Daaimah Jardin, 2023

My Beginnings

Chapter 1
Who am I?

P rimarily, I want to honor my ancestors by giving you a brief history of my father's family. I know my father's side of the family better than I know my mother's.

Calvin Jordan (my grandfather) and Laura Gray (my grandmother) started the Jordan Family in Starkville, Mississippi, and later moved to DB Turner Plantation, in Ruleville, Sunflower County, Mississippi. The plantation was owned and operated by Turner who had a brother named David Turner. The plantation was located West of Ruleville and adjoined to Dockery Plantation. It is now a farm called Turner Place and owned by Eric Shuster.

Calvin Jordan and Laura Gray started the Jordan family in the late 1800s. Calvin was born about 1852 in South Carolina, and Laura was born about 1857 in Virginia.

Records show that there were two Jordan enslavers in Oktibbeha, and one owned Calvin. According to the documentation, they were the last generation of our family in slavery.

In February 2005 at a genealogy workshop in Los Angeles, a genealogist helped me locate my paternal grandmother in the 1870 Census. She was 16 years old and living in the house with her parents, William and Eliza Gray, and seven other siblings, all of whom were Black, except Laura whose race was "Mulatto" and a part of the Choctaw Agency. This led me to believe that William, the father in the Gray's household, was not Laura's biological father, but she was the child of a slave master. This blatant disrespect infuriated me.

Calvin and Laura Jordan started rearing their children in Starkville, Oktibbeha County, Mississippi. They had eleven living children and one who passed away before being named. Records show that the first four were born in Oktibbeha County. They moved from Starkville to Indianola and then to Ruleville, rural Sunflower County, where they raised their family.

Calvin and Laura's first child, **John**, was born in 1874 and passed away in 1969. John never married and did not have any children.

Eliza, the second child, was born in 1876. She married Robert Johnson, and they had six children, two daughters and four sons. Eliza named her first daughter Irene, after her sister. Irene married at an early age and is the granddaughter of Sandra Bingham, who gave me this information.

Irene was the third child. She was born in 1877. She married and had three sons. Irene and her husband were students at Tuskegee; she later became a school principal. She and her family moved to Troy, Alabama, Pike County, where she and her husband became professors at higher learning institutions.

Lena, the fourth child, was born in 1879. Her whereabouts are unknown.

Leland, the fifth child, was born in 1880. He married Matilda Anderson, and they had ten children. Uncle Leland fascinated me, because I knew five of his ten children, including his only daughter, who has one son and two daughters. Because Uncle Leland's sons look so much alike, I could envision their father. In addition to Uncle Leland's ten children, he had 130 grandchildren, 154 great-grandchildren, and twenty-one great-great-grandchildren as of 2014. What a man!

William was the sixth child. He was born in 1880. He married Nancy, and they had four children. There is no additional information about Uncle William and his family.

Unnamed - The seventh child passed away before being named.

Mary, the eighth child, was born in 1895. She married Anthony Rand, and they did not have any children. They stayed at 33rd and State Street in the Mecca building in Chicago, Illinois. After Uncle Anthony passed away, Aunt Mary moved in with her brother, Lovelace, and his family. Later she moved to Troy, Alabama to live with her sister, Irene, and her family. Aunt Mary passed away in the 1940s in Pike County, Alabama.

Clement was the ninth child. His whereabouts are unknown.

Calvin II, the tenth child, and my father was born about 1891. He married my mother, Georgia Mack, and they had twelve children, seven sons and five daughters. Detailed information regarding both of my parents is coming.

Lovelace, the youngest son of Calvin and Laura Jordan. Uncle Lovelace, whom we called Uncle Love, was born on July 4, 1898. He was married twice and had seventeen children; four with his first wife, two of whom perished in a house fire. Uncle Love and his second wife, Aunt Alice, had thirteen children. Additionally, he had forty-seven grandchildren, forty-four great-grandchildren, and nine great-great-grandchildren.

Ms. Willie Shipp is Calvin and Laura Jordan's last child, born in 1897. She married Simon Shipp, and they had five children, thirty-five grandchildren, thirty-eight great-grandchildren, and forty-eight great-great-grandchildren. Aunt Willie lived her entire life in Ruleville, Mississippi. She passed away in 1998.

Note: After 1933, my father's last name was changed from Jordan to Jardan by Fard Muhammad.

Chapter 2
My Father, Calvin Jordan II, And His Family

I do not recall my father talking much about his parents or siblings, and I never really thought about it until I started doing genealogy research. Sadly, by then, it was too late because he was already deceased. However, my mother talked about her family.

In my family history research, I discovered that my father registered in 1917 for the army. However, records show that he did not serve in the military. He was not in the household in the 1920 Census, and my mother was the head of the family, living in Arkansas. Therefore, I believe that he might have been looking for another location to relocate. My father moved to several southern states until he moved to Illinois in 1930 where he became a member of the Nation of Islam.

My father was a sturdy, hardworking, no-nonsense person who provided for, and protected his family. I knew his youngest brother, Uncle Lovelace, whom as I mentioned, we called Uncle Love.

Uncle Love and his family also lived in Chicago, near where we lived. I knew my father had two sisters, Aunt Mary, older than him, and Aunt Willie, younger. Uncle Love was a preacher, and my father was a member of the Nation of Islam, which created tension. Uncle Love enjoyed coming to our house to antagonize my father until my father put him out.

My father worked long hours because he did not have a regular job. Consequently, he did not spend much time at home. He had a pushcart until he could afford to purchase an old truck to pick up junk, which he took to the junkyard to sell. He brought home some of the items so we could use them. The length of time he worked might have depended on the money he needed for a particular day. I really cannot say.

On one Sunday in 1943, the police went to the temple in Chicago and temples in other cities and arrested all the brothers who were not disabled, including my father and oldest brother. My father was almost 48 years old.

My father and eldest brother, Farroz, were incarcerated in an institution in Sandstone, Minnesota. If there was anything good about their incarceration, it was the fact that they were both in the same institution; hence, my mother only had to make one trip. My mother took me to see them once; however, I cried so much that she never took me again. She also took my brother, Calvin III.

In this prison, the inmates were required to learn a skill. My father learned needlework and made assorted items for his family, but unfortunately, we lost them.

Some of the brothers, who were considered disabled or too old, were not arrested. One of those brothers was Brother John Hassan, another was Brother Ephram Bahar.

While the brothers were away from home, the sisters and their families moved together, for security reasons. My mother, two of my teenage sisters, my youngest brother, and I moved with

Sister Katie and her family. She and her family lived downstairs in a two-story flat, and we lived upstairs.

The Honorable Elijah Muhammad, and at least one of his sons, were also arrested. When his wife, Sister Clara Muhammad, visited him, she would bring information back to the members.

The sisters and children did not attend the Temple when the brothers were away from home. However, we did go to school with various sisters' families. One of those sisters was Sister Ada. She lived over a garage, and you had to enter her house through the alley. After the brothers returned from prison, we purchased another temple and continued with our schooling.

When the brothers were finally released, my father got us a house, and we moved. We lived in a place on the south side of Chicago, but not as far west as we lived before my father left.

Shortly after the brothers returned home, the Honorable Elijah Muhammad sent my father to manage the Nation of Islam's first farm in White Cloud, Michigan. White Cloud, MI is approximately 221 miles from Chicago, IL. It is in the Midwest, and like most Midwestern cities, the weather is hot and humid during the summer months and cold and almost unbearable during the fall and winter months.

Like most homes in rural areas, our house did not have running water or inside toilets. Using the restroom in the winter months was brutal. My mother and I frequently used a slop bucket in the winter months, and Papa dumped it for us.

During the planting and harvesting seasons, brothers from Chicago assisted my father with planting fruits and vegetables. They also helped harvest the produce in the late summer and early fall. They took some of the products back to Chicago to sell in the Nation of Islam stores.

We also had cows, sheep, goats, and chickens on the farm. My father did not have a lot of success breeding some of the cattle. I remember one cow who was unable to deliver her calf. The cow either passed away, or my father had to put the cow to sleep. I did not like goats because they would run behind you and bump into you with their heads. Sometimes my father would let us help him milk the cows. We drank some of the milk, and when the milk went sour, Mama put the milk in a churner, which is a big crock pot, and used a large stick with a small ball on the end to beat the milk until it became butter and buttermilk.

White Cloud had an annual season for hunting deer. Before and after the season, deer came right up to our doors; however, they never ventured so close during the hunting season. They must have sensed the danger. Not that Papa did not try, but the deer never came.

Once, my father was trying to repair a tractor when the fan belt came off and cut his face just below his ear to almost his lip. He put his hand on his face to stop the bleeding but did not flinch. He was so strong. The only time I saw my father cry was when he lost one of his brothers. I do not know which brother he lost at that time, but I do not remember my father crying when he lost his youngest brother, Uncle Love, in 1959.

Sometimes Papa sat on the couch, and Calvin III and I would sit on the floor close to his feet, and he would entertain us by telling us things like the following story:

It was on one Sunday morning that the preacher went out hunting. He forgot all about his religion, and he carried his shotgun along. On his way home, he killed a few quails and a fine hare (rabbit). On his way back home, he met a grizzly bear. The bear started walking up to the preacher, and the preacher climbed up a cinnamon tree. He got to the top of the tree, crawled out on a limb, and cast his eyes to the G-d in the sky; this is what he said to Him: "Oh Lord, you heard Daniel in the lion's den, also Brother Jonah in the whale's belly. You heard the Hebrew children in the fire of a furnace and the excellent book declares that, please put a muzzle on this bear!"

Papa never told us fairy tales.

When Papa was angry or upset about something, he would say, "Goddamn the luck to hell." He was also fond of reading the *Islam Problem Book.* One of his favorite passages said, "Each Muslim was required to bring the head of four devils. By getting and presenting the four at one time, his reward was a visit to the Holy City of Mecca to see Fard Muhammad."

We stayed in White Cloud from 1946 to 1949, then moved back to Illinois, but not to Chicago. My father told the Honorable Elijah Muhammad that he was getting too old to handle the farm and needed a replacement, and the Honorable Elijah Muhammad found a replacement. Meantime, mother, and I stayed in White Cloud with the replacement family until my father found housing for us.

While driving from White Cloud, Michigan, to Illinois, Papa's truck broke down. He and my sister, Geneva, were stranded until Papa had the vehicle repaired. My father found and rented part of a house in St. Anne, Illinois, owned by a lady who was not living there. I do not remember how long we stayed in that house, but Papa found us another place close to where we lived, but not as lovely. However, we had use of the entire house.

Papa eventually purchased a lot with two structures on it. Uncle Love's son, Edward, helped my father convert one of the facilities into a living area and the other into a kitchen.

Soon after that, Papa started farming again, but not on the scale he did in White Cloud. He only planted watermelon and vegetables and raised a few chickens. We lived about sixty miles from Chicago; therefore, on Saturdays, Papa took his produce to Chicago and sold them to the Muslims who lived there. They would be waiting for those red, ripe, juicy sweet watermelons.

Papa also worked for the railroad, but I am not sure in what capacity. Additionally, he did odd jobs for a Caucasian man in Indiana until young male Caucasians became jealous and started harassing him.

My father got sick between 1958 and 1959 while I was still living in Chicago and working for the Nation of Islam. Papa resided in St. Ann, Illinois, but the hospital was in Chicago. I told the Honorable Elijah Muhammad about my father's hospitalization, and he visited my father and gave him a substantial amount of money for his hospitalization expenses. Now that I remember my father's symptoms, I believe he might have had prostate cancer; however, he lived until he was in his late seventies.

Chapter 3
My Mother, Georgia Mack
(Mack Pearson)

Mama was a small, gentle, kind, caring, and peaceful person. She was also a spotless person as well as an excellent cook. As an adult and a mother, I had compassion for her. In those days, girls married at an early age. I estimate that my mother got married at about sixteen; she had her first child when she was about seventeen and her last child when she was thirty-eight. She gave birth to twelve children over 21 years.

Her third child, Arthur Calvin, passed away at an early age. Mama's ninth child, Willie, passed away in my sister Georgia's lap. I knew my last brother, Leroy, passed away when he was a teenager; he loved me and called me 'Losee.' He sent me a box of candy from the hospital, and I kept the empty box.

Georgia said he passed away from an accident when the jack holding the car he was repairing slipped and fell on him. My sister said that my mother had just returned from the hospital, a long distance from our house, visiting him, and she had to return to the hospital, because he passed away.

Unlike my father, my mother talked about her family. Her father's name was George Mack, and her mother's name was Maggie Mack or Magdalene Mack Pearson. My mother had two brothers and one sister. Her brothers were Arthur and Andy. Arthur was the eldest, and Andy was the youngest child.

My mother's sister, Clara, was the second child, and my mother was the third child.

My mother and many sisters, who were followers of the Honorable Elijah Muhammad, refused to send their children to public school. They protested, and the police arrested them. At that time, my mother was pregnant with me. Folks, parents protesting the school system is NOT new!

My mother worked on the Northside of Chicago as a domestic cleaner, cleaning homes for Caucasians, which enabled her to care for us. Several of us would go to the market on the weekend with Mama. She purchased live chickens and had them slaughtered. She also bought white navy beans, whole wheat flour, and rice in bulk. Of course, we ate our white bean soup, browned white rice, homemade bread with freshly churned buttermilk, and hot rolls with melted butter. I can still taste them now.

In addition to working five and sometimes 5 1/2 days per week, the women visited the sick sisters, took them food, and occasionally gave them small cash donations.

When we lived in White Cloud, my mother and I seldom went to the grocery store. My father and my brother Calvin III did most of the shopping. She did most of the cooking; however, I would help Mama churn the milk. When she stirred the milk, she sometimes would say, ***"Do, do come butter do, old man Lazarus sitting at the gate waiting for the butter so, do, do, do come butter do."***

My mother also said some sage things like, "You know where you have been, but you do not know where you are going."

And, "You do not know on whose pillow you will have to lie your head."

My Mother's Close Friends

Sister Leona

My mother had several close friends. One of them was Sister Leona. She and my mother were like biological sisters. Sister Leona and her husband, Brother John, lived upstairs in one of the Nation of Islam's commercial and residential buildings on 71st Street, west of Cottage Grove.

Cottage Grove was one of the main streets on the south side of Chicago, where many Afro-Americans lived in the 50s and 60s.

The first floor was commercial, and the second floor was residential. Sister Leona had one adult son from a previous marriage, who lived in Altadena, California, where she and her husband later moved. She was an immaculate housekeeper and an excellent cook. Her house was so clean that you did not want to walk on her floors.

Years later, Sister Leona and her husband moved to California to live with her son. While living in California, her husband became ill and had to live in a convalescent facility. I went to see him at least once, and he passed away there.

Sister Leona had hip replacement surgery. The medical staff let her fall out of the bed, and after that she was terrified. I went to see her as often as I could. My husband at that time, Riza, was the Imam in Pasadena. When I was on vacation during the summer months, I would ride the bus from Los Angeles to Pasadena to spend some time with her and ride back with Riza after the Wednesday night meeting.

Although Sister Leona had someone to assist her with cooking, cleaning, and personal needs, I knew how meticulous she was about certain things, especially food and cleanliness. Therefore, occasionally, when I visited her, I cooked for her.

Between the yolk and white part of a raw egg is a stringy part of the egg that most people never notice; but she did. She did not like that part of the egg and would ask me to remove it. Once I removed that part, she would be so pleased.

It is amazing how small things can make some people so happy. Making people happy and achieving their goals also makes me happy. She also had a sense of humor. Her home was tranquil and peaceful; hence, after I drove or rode to her house and sat down for a few minutes, I sometimes went to sleep. When I would awaken, she would say, "it is a good thing that there are no flies in this house."

Sister Leona gave me about six white hand towels with green floral trimming close to the bottom. For years, I did not use those towels; however, I started using them as I got older.

Occasionally, believers from Chicago visited Los Angeles. If I knew the person also knew Sister Leona, I would take the person to see her. Once, Sister Frances, the longtime cook for Sister Clara and the Honorable Elijah Muhammad, visited California, and I took her to visit Sister Leona, which was enjoyable for both.

I tried to visit her daily during feeding hours because they fed her intravenously unless someone was there to feed her. Inserting and replacing the feed tube is painful, and I wanted to minimize her pain. Being near her and trying to make her comfortable was a pleasure for me since I could not do the same for my mother.

Sister Leona was living in California with her son when my mother passed away. She cried when I called her and told her that my mother had passed away. When I went to Chicago for my mother's funeral, she sent a fruit basket.

When Sister Leona passed away, her son cremated her. I have only talked or spoken to him once since his mother passed away, and his whereabouts are unknown to me.

Sister Leotha

Sister Leotha was another one of my mother's good friends. I do not remember her being married; however, I do remember that she had a daughter.

She lived on the second or third floor of an apartment building on the south side of Chicago. I just remember walking up all those stairs to visit her. She was small and, as I remember, a quiet person. She made the best gingerbread that I have ever eaten.

Honestly, I still remember the taste of that gingerbread after more than sixty years. I did not have the same interactions with Sister Leotha I had with Sister Leona.

Sister Sharrieff

Like my parents, Sister Maggie Sharrieff followed the Honorable Elijah from the inception. Fard Muhammad gave her the last name of Sharrieff. She lived in the same Nation of Islam building where Sister Leona lived. She was very witty. One of her favorite sayings was, "You live, and you learn, and you die, and you forget all about it." She was a sweet little sister, who I could not wait to outgrow, and I did.

May Allah bless all these sisters with Paradise!

Chapter 4
My Siblings

Maggie

My parents' first child and my oldest sister, Magdalene, who we called Maggie, was born about 1915 in Mississippi. Her name was the same as our maternal grandmother, and I have learned that naming your first female child after your mother is a southern tradition. Maggie was grown and out of the house when I was born.

Maggie seemed humble and sad, and I heard she lived for a brief time with one of my father's sisters, Aunt Mary, who I barely knew, and my father's new religion was not her preference.

Maggie married William Graham, whom we called Bill. Unfortunately, Bill drank on the weekends, and he was also abusive. They had two children, a son and a daughter, William Graham Jr., and Blanche. Maggie's children and I grew up together, and I was four and six years older than they were. Not only was Maggie my oldest sister, but I also thought of her as a second mother since she was 20 years older than I. She took me to amusement parks and the zoo with her children when we were young. Her children completed high school and attended institutions of higher learning.

My nephew had a son named Tony when he was about nineteen. Of course, like many young men, he denied the child. When he was about two or three years old, Maggie had a picture of William when Tony was about that age and Maggie placed a picture of Tony near William; the resemblance was undeniable. Maggie loved Tony.

William Jr. married a lady named Ruby, and we called her Ruby D. They had three children: two sons and one daughter. She was a loving, kind, caring wife and mother, an excellent housekeeper, and a seamstress. Ruby and my sister Beatrice were good friends.

My nephew, whom we call Graham, and Ruby both worked to provide a comfortable family lifestyle. Graham worked in Law Enforcement for many years.

Since I did not live in Chicago for about nine years, Graham, Blanche, and I did not spend much of our childhood together. I did not live in Chicago from 1946-1955. By the time I returned, everyone was almost grown.

I went to Chicago several days before attending one of my nephews' weddings with fabric and pattern in hand, and Ruby made my dress for me. Unfortunately, Ruby and a friend of hers were killed in an automobile accident while returning to Chicago from visiting Ruby's daughter at Iowa State University. That was a sad occasion for all of us. William and Ruby have several grandchildren.

For many years after Ruby's death, Graham said he would not remarry. However, he finally remarried a lady with a small daughter, and they stayed married until she passed away about four or five years ago.

Graham also lost one of his sons to a heart attack. His son came home from work, sat down, and passed away. Graham lives in Chicago during the summer and Las Vegas during the winter months.

Previously, he had a summer home in Puerto Rico, but he sold that home and purchased another summer home in Las Vegas.

After his second wife passed away, he remarried because he had diabetes and glaucoma and needed assistance with daily living activities.

On November 15, 2019, a friend of mine from Los Angeles, California, drove me to Las Vegas to celebrate his 80-birthday party. I enjoyed seeing him since the last time I saw him was at a family reunion in Kankakee, Illinois, in July of 2012. However, we talked occasionally.

I enjoyed seeing him, although he looked frail. He passed away in 2020, and we miss him. May G-d forgive him for all his bad deeds and accept all his honorable deeds. Ameen.

Blanche, Maggie's daughter, my oldest niece, and good friend, grew to be a beautiful young girl and lady. She was like a younger sister to me.

When I returned to Chicago in 1955, I stayed there for five years before moving to California. Blanche and I spent quality time together whenever I visited Chicago.

Blanche started her career at the University of Chicago in the ROTC Department as a clerk and attended classes in the evening. She remained at the University of Chicago for thirty years until she retired. She advanced from clerical to an administrative position before she retired.

Blanche married Joe, and they had three children, two daughters, and one son: Sabrina, Debbie, and Shawn, the youngest. Unfortunately, Blanche and Joe divorced when the children were young, and she became a single parent.

My sister Maggie, Blanche's mother, helped Blanche as much as she could, even though Maggie was not in the best of health. Joe's mother also helped with the children. However, since she lived in Milwaukee, Wisconsin, and Blanche lived in Chicago, Illinois, she could only help on weekends or school vacations. Somehow, Blanche survived. Blanche's children were well-behaved, very obedient, disciplined, and did well in school.

Blanche's health had been declining, and I wanted to spend quality time with her; therefore, when I was in Chicago in 2010 for a family reunion, I spent several days helping her clean the way she liked. I was also able to cook her some good greens. I was thankful that Allah (G-d) allowed me to spend that time with her because she passed away on December 29, 2010.

After graduating from Dunbar Vocational High School in Chicago, Illinois, Sabrina attended Iowa State University, where she received her Bachelor's in 1990. Later, she earned her master's degree from Nebraska University.

Sabrina got married and had a child who passed away in infancy. She and her first husband divorced, and she remarried Willie Herman, an outstanding man who lived in Allen, Texas.

He had a daughter about ten years old with his first wife. His daughter stayed with them occasionally. His daughter and Sabrina got along very well because Sabrina was caring and kind and took loving care of her.

Several years after marrying Willie, Sabrina became ill, and the doctors had difficulty diagnosing her illness. When they finally diagnosed her, the diagnosis was lupus; after that, she was in and out of the hospital.

I would call Sabrina's mother, Blanche, frequently to check on Sabrina's condition. One day in December of 2006, it dawned on me that I had not talked to Sabrina for about a year. Her mother had left Chicago and gone to Texas to be with Sabrina, and all that time, I had not been to see either one of them. I immediately called Blanche, apologized for my thoughtlessness, and told her I would come. She suggested I wait until after Christmas because Willie Herman's family visited them during Christmas. I immediately made reservations for January 6, 2007, as I prayed to Allah to keep her until I saw her again, and He answered my prayer.

Since Willie and Sabrina lived in Allen, Texas, and there is no airport in Allen, you can fly into Dallas or Fort Worth. Blanche told me to fly to Dallas, Texas because it is closer to Allen than Fort Worth. Blanche picked me up at the airport, and we drove to Allen. I rested for a brief time, then we went to the hospital to visit Sabrina, who was delighted to see me.

Willie went to see Sabrina on his way home from work, and Blanche went during the afternoon. Willie went to see Sabrina every day while she was hospitalized, except when he went out of town to his daughter's track meet. Now can you see why he will always be my nephew? Although I had talked to Willie Herman several times on the telephone, I had not seen him. It was a pleasure to see him when he returned home that evening.

While I was in Texas, when Willie arrived at the hospital, he called Blanche to inform her that Sabrina's blood pressure was shallow. Blanche and I immediately left the house and went to the hospital. By the time we arrived, Sabrina's pressure had improved slightly. I became very emotional and almost cried, but Blanche was very calm. She reminded me that her own mother had had a prolonged illness before she passed away.

After Sabrina was in the hospital for a year-plus, she improved. Therefore, she went to an extended care facility but had to return to the hospital.

To compound her illness, Sabrina had kidney failure and had to go on dialysis, I believe daily, for many hours. Blanche told me that Sabrina told her, "Mama, I am tired." Sabrina's illness was taxing on her husband, parents, and siblings. She passed away about a month after I left Texas. Besides Sabrina's father, Blanche's brother Graham, her two remaining children, and their spouses, my sister Beatrice, my nephew Freeman, Willie Herman's family, and daughter who attended the funeral to support Blanche; she held up well.

Blanche's second child, Debbie, was a beautiful little girl who grew up to be a beautiful and talented woman. She also attended elementary and secondary schools in Chicago and still resides in a suburban area of Chicago. She is an excellent seamstress.

The clothes she makes look like the ones you see the models wearing in Vogue Magazine. She can decorate a house from the window coverings to the couch and pillow coverings.

Deborah is married to Curtis Bankhead, and they have two sons. The oldest son is 17 years old, and the youngest is 12 years old.

They are outstanding parents. Their boys are well mannered, well-behaved, and active in sports. They play different sports at separate times and locations. Debbie ensures they get to all their games and practices on time while Curtis takes care of everything else.

Shawn (Jordan) Thompson, Blanche's youngest child, attended elementary and secondary schools in Chicago. Jordan has six children, two with his first wife and four with his second wife: currently, Jordan and his second family live in Northern California.

Trazse

My parent's second child was born Trazse, but Fard Muhammad, who came from the Middle East and taught the Honorable Elijah Muhammad, changed his first name to Farroz, but he did not change his last name, Jordan, our family name.

Farroz was born around 1918 in the state of Tennessee. I assume that he was between 14 and 15 when our father became a member of the Nation of Islam; therefore, I do not know whether he attended public school or for how long. However, as a young man, he was knowledgeable. He loved to eat and always called Mama, Sister Georgia.

When we lived on the Nation of Islam farm, Farroz came from Chicago with the brothers and helped with planting and harvesting the products. Sometimes a brother would get a dictionary and select words for Farroz to define, and he seldom missed a definition. I was in the house near them where they could not see me, and I was extremely impressed. Recently, I reflected that he might have spent much time studying in prison.

Shortly before he went to prison, Farroz married a beautiful young lady named Idonia. She had tuberculosis and passed away while he was away, and he was not allowed to come home for her funeral. When he heard the news of her death, he said he expected her death, but it was still painful.

Farroz and my brother Calvin III, were the only two of Papa's sons who spent some time in the Nation of Islam. Farroz was a teacher at the University of Islam in Chicago, and Imam Warith Deen Muhammad, as well as Darnell Karim, were some of his students. He also worked in one of the Nation of Islam's bakeries.

Among his friends were Captain Raymond Sharrief who was married to the Honorable Elijah's oldest daughter, Ethel Muhammad. Captain Sharrief had two brothers, Alfonso Pasha and Kaska Ali that were also married. Farroz lived in one of Alfonso Pasha's apartment buildings on 62nd and Drexel in Chicago.

A Sister in the Nation of Islam admired Farroz; however, he did not marry her. He married a lady named Arlene, who had a twin sister, Pauline. Arlene also had a young daughter, Marlene, and she and Farroz had two sons, Farroz Jr. and Steven. Farroz Jr. is deceased, and we do not know the whereabouts of Steven. I am unaware of any biological grandchildren Farroz has, but Marlene has several children. Farroz passed away in 1987. His widow, Arlene Jordan, passed away in November 2015.

Arthur Calvin

According to the 1920 Census, Arthur Calvin was born in Hampstead, Arkansas. He was named after my mother's oldest brother and my father, and he passed away in infancy. I wondered why my father had six sons before naming one Calvin, and now I know.

Richard

Richard, aka Blue, was the fourth child and third son. He was born around 1921 in Arkansas. According to the 1930 Census, Richard attended school and could read and write. In the 1940 Census, he was no longer in the house with us. He worked as a security guard.

He was a heavy drinker and infrequently came to the house. When he visited the house, he wanted to hug me, which I resisted because I disliked alcohol.

As a young Muslim child, I was wearing a long dress and recall seeing Richard. He looked at me and said, "What is that you have on, baby?" I looked at him, laughed, talked to him for a few minutes, and left. After we moved to White Cloud and back to Illinois, I do not remember seeing Richard, and I do not believe he came to Papa's funeral.

To my knowledge, Richard never married or had any children. My brother Calvin III told me that Richard had several girlfriends during his lifetime. Additionally, he said that Richard slept with one eye open, and he was a guy that you did not play with or cross.

He passed away in 1970, shortly after he stopped drinking.

Mama had to see another one of her sons buried. At that time, I was living in California, and I did not attend his funeral.

Leon

Leon was the fourth son, also known as the "Bird that must be heard." He was one of my mother's favorite sons. He loved spaghetti, and Mama had to cook spaghetti for him and my sister

Georgia. Mama referred to Leon and Georgia as her 'yellow children.' He came over frequently to see Mama and us.

Leon also worked, and when we moved back to Illinois, he and my brother Calvin III went to the farm to help Papa with the farm work, and they boxed and wrestled.

He was about 9 or 10 years old when Papa became a member of the Nation of Islam. Therefore, I do not know if or whether he attended public school. I am sure that if he lived in Papa's house that he would go to the Temple.

Leon lived with a lady named Lillie who had a little daughter. He never married or had children. Unfortunately, a man killed Leon in January 1962 because of a $5.00 gambling dispute. Some years later, my niece, Blanche, told me my mother started declining after Leon's death.

Georgia

My sister Georgia, named after my mother, a southern tradition, was my parents' second daughter and sixth child. She was gregarious and loved being around people. Everyone knew she was in the house because they got a warm greeting and a hug. She loved to sing; I understand she had a beautiful voice when she was young and wanted to become an entertainer. I remember Lottie Muhammad, the daughter of the Honorable Elijah Muhammad, once asked me about Georgia. She and Georgia were close in age and grew up together. She told me that she liked Georgia. There are very few people who did not like Georgia. Papa was one of those because she said to me that Papa wanted to put her out of the house, but Mama would not let him. She was married once and had a daughter who passed away in infancy.

Again, I am not aware of her educational background. For many years, she worked in nightclubs; in her later years, she worked in a laundry and was a caregiver.

In 2012, doctors diagnosed Georgia with throat cancer and gave her about six months to live; however, she lived for three additional years. Even though she had not attended the Temple or the Masjid since childhood, she started talking about Allah, and He knew best when she would die.

Therefore, I decided she should have a Muslim burial when she passed away. I knew whom I would ask to perform the ceremony, my childhood friend, Darnell Karim, who lived in Chicago. Additionally, Darnell's wife, Gloria's oldest sister, and my sister grew up together. Darnell, Gloria, and Gloria's oldest sister all attended the funeral.

My niece in Chicago and I prepared the obituary. I did not attend because it was early in April, and I was not going to Chicago in April when the weather was still cold. My daughter and I sent our support.

Since my granddaughters knew and loved their Aunt Georgia, I asked them to contribute to the service. My oldest granddaughter said she would contribute, but that ended when it was time for her to part with her money.

Leroy

Leroy was my parents' fifth son. I do not know why, but he was my favorite brother. Perhaps because he played with me a lot or sent me a box of candy from the hospital before he passed away, and I kept the empty container for many years. Whatever the reason, I always thought of him as my favorite brother.

Calvin III said Leroy helped Papa repair a car when the jack holding the vehicle slipped or broke and fell on him. He was hospitalized but did not survive his injuries.

Geneva

Geneva is the third daughter and the eighth child of my parents.

She resembled Papa. One of my first cousins always told her, "Geneva, you look just like Uncle Calvin," which is true. She always complained about Papa not letting her attend public school; she attended the University of Islam for a while. She attended Temple #2 in Chicago until 1975. She could almost quote the Honorable Elijah Muhammad's speeches verbatim.

When the brothers were away and Mama was at work, Geneva took care of my brother Calvin III and me. When she finished washing the clothes, she would put us in the same water and bathe us.

After my maternal grandmother passed away, my mother's sister, Aunt Clara, left Mississippi and came to Chicago to live. She stayed with us while Papa was still in jail, and we were not kind to her, especially my two older sisters, Geneva, and Beatrice.

Geneva began working for the rich and famous on the north side of Chicago (also known as the Gold Coast) at an early age. Her employers took her to their summer home in Lake Haven, a city close to Chicago, to clean and babysit during vacation.

On the first anniversary of my late husband, Ronald T. Stokes' death, Geneva came from Chicago to Los Angeles to be with me. While she was here, she thought it would be good to have Brother William 12X, who was shot and paralyzed when Ronald was killed, over for dinner on the weekend. Since Brother

William had not started driving, brothers lined up to bring him to the house to have an enjoyable meal weekly. Geneva was generous.

While Geneva was in California, she met one of my friends, Sister Denise. She liked Geneva, and they had a lot in common, and she loved Geneva's cooking. I almost lost one of my good friends to my sister.

When Imam Muhammad became the leader of the former Nation of Islam, Geneva asked Riza, my husband, to help her select a Muslim name, and he did. Riza asked me some of her characteristics that enabled him to choose a name. When I told him, he selected Karima; she loved the name and used it until she passed away.

Geneva was married twice and had a son from her first marriage, Clarence Junior, a typical boy, very naughty. He even thought he could fly, and he tried it once, broke his arm and learned the results. Clarence settled down, made it through elementary and secondary school, and got a job at the post office where he still works.

Clarence Junior had a son who has seven children and seven grandchildren; his daughter has one grown son.

He later married, and he and his wife had a son, who is also grown. They also adopted a daughter.

Clarence lives in a south suburban area of Chicago, where he has a beautiful home and some apartment units.

Willie

My parents' sixth son, Willie, born in 1932, also passed away as an infant. My sister Georgia told me she was holding him when he passed away, and I do not remember asking her how old he was when he passed away; therefore, I do not have that information.

Beatrice

Beatrice is my parents' fourth daughter and tenth child. She is five years older than I, and we have been together more than my other sisters. She also attended the University of Islam. When we moved to White Cloud, Michigan, she came with us. She did not like being in the country. She was always whining, crying, and complaining. Papa got tired of her behavior, and my brother Calvin III said that one night, Papa told me to pack her bags. The following day, Papa took Bea to the train station and sent her to Chicago to live with a sister who had a daughter close to her age. She was the same sister with whom we lived when Papa was in jail. Bea loved that arrangement.

She stayed with that sister and her family until Geneva got an apartment; then, she moved with Geneva. She also stayed with two different cousins and their families.

Bea started working at an early age. She worked in a drug store with a snack bar and a factory. When she came home from work, she talked on the telephone to her coworkers while cooking, cleaning, and doing whatever else she had to do. After working with someone all day, I could not understand what else she needed to discuss.

She eventually started doing domestic work. Toward the end of her working years, she worked for one of Hunt's descendants. Yes, Hunt's Tomatoes and other products, and he still sends her a retirement check annually.

Beatrice, whom we call Bea, married James Fair, and they have five children, three sons and two daughters, eight grandchildren, and three great-grandchildren.

I called James Fair, "brother" because he was like another brother to me. He was genuinely kind with a beautiful smile to go with his beautiful teeth.

Bea's oldest son, Freeman, my favorite nephew, is considerate and generous. He lived with my parents and me in Illinois when he was young. He recently told me that my father told him, "Son, get an education to avoid working as hard as I have done."

Freeman attended public schools in Chicago and applied himself; he graduated in 1969. He attended Elmhurst College, located in a northwest suburban area of Chicago near O'Hara Airport. Freeman wanted to pursue a medical career, worked hard, took classes that guided him in that direction, and earned good grades. He graduated from Elmhurst in 1973.

Then he attended Loyola Stritch School of Medicine in Illinois from 1973 to 1977. At this institution, he encountered some discouragement from a dean who told him that he knew there was a need for doctors in his community, but he did not believe that Freeman could become a doctor. The dean suggested that he would help him find a job or why not become a teacher.

Freeman told the dean that he came to Loyola to become a doctor and did precisely that. The dean's statements and what my father told him made him more determined to succeed by graduating in 1977.

He worked for US Public Health Services in a medically underserved area in East Chicago Heights, Illinois from 1980 to

1983, which paid for three of the four years of his medical school education.

Freeman met Brendetta Pruitt when they were students at Elmhurst College. She lived with her parents and younger brother Earl Lee, Jr. in Maywood, Illinois, close to Elmhurst. Brendetta was a candid individual. She was an ambitious young lady, an excellent cook, and a leader, and she loved Freeman.

Her mother, a retired teacher, was an affectionate person who enjoyed traveling. When she retired, she traveled across the United States and internationally. She also played chess on the internet with people worldwide. Mrs. Pruitt loved hats and had many beautiful ones, which she wore well.

Brendetta's father was a pleasant gentleman who loved traveling in their motor home. He was a manager for Campbell Soup Company. Her brother was younger than her; he worked for United Airlines and was quiet. They were an enjoyable family.

Freeman and Brendetta got married on August 18, 1979. Both family members and a host of friends attended the extravagant event.

They had a son, Freeman III, on June 14, 1983, whom the grandparents adored. As a small child, Freeman III traveled frequently with his grandparents. He had a pillow he took with him everywhere he went. If his parents forgot the pillow, they had to return and get it. He even took the pillow to college with him.

The family moved to San Antonio, TX, in November of 1983, where Freeman became employed as a pediatrician at the Pediatric Medical Group, where he still works. Being the friendly person that she was, Brendetta quickly made friends in the Church and elsewhere.

Brendetta and Freeman adopted newborn identical twin girls, Sibbieo and Elaina, in 1991. They were adorable, and they completed their family. Brendetta was a stay-at-home mother; everyone loved her and helped her with her choices.

Mr. Pruitt, unfortunately, passed away in 1992 while he was outdoors watering the lawn. The hose started watering the window, and Mrs. Pruitt thought he was his playful self until a neighbor knocked on the door and told her that he was on the ground. On the way to the hospital, the paramedic could not resuscitate him. When Freeman III learned his grandfather had passed away, he could not understand why his father, a doctor, could not have prevented his grandfather's death.

After Mr. Pruitt's death, Mrs. Pruitt spent the summers in Chicago and Texas in the winters with Freeman and Brendetta. Mrs. Pruitt had a motor home which she kept in a mobile park in San Antonio when she was there. The motor home was plush and comfortable. I stayed in the motor home with her for one or two nights when visiting Freeman and Brendetta.

As time passed and the children grew older, Brendetta assumed more responsibility. She enrolled the children in extracurricular activities, including Jack and Jill, and was president of Jack and Jill of America, Inc., in Texas.

I visited Freeman and Brendetta once when they lived in their first home. She knew where all the bargain shopping areas were, and we went to them. I saw a tamale pie recipe in one of her cookbooks, copied it, took it home, and prepared it many times. Everyone loved the tamale pie.

When Freeman and Brendetta initially moved to Texas, they lived in an apartment for several years. Then they bought a house in a new subdivision, lived there for about seven years, and later had a two-story house with a huge basement built. Brendetta participated in designing the home.

I loved that house. A three-car garage was in the rear of the house, including a recreation room, a small bathroom with a toilet, shower, and a hair shampoo bowl. There was a large storage area with shelves and stairways which took you directly upstairs into the kitchen.

You entered the first level of the house into the foyer with a closet for guests' coats as well as a dining area. Down a couple of stairs was a small front room. The front room was on the right side of the aisle, and the dining room on the left, both beautifully decorated. A half bath was on the left side of the hall. Then you entered a large family room on the right side with ample cabinets and shelves for family portraits and electronics.

You stepped out of the family room through a door, onto a deck with an umbrella-covered swing. Next to the family room was a gourmet kitchen, a walk-in pantry, and a laundry room. A huge primary bedroom suite was on the first level.

The stairways to the second level were in the hallway. A large media, recreational room, four bedrooms, and two bathrooms were on the second level. I visited them in their new home several months after it was completed. We had a family reunion in Texas in 1994.

Freeman III played soccer, basketball, and football in high school. Time went by quickly, and Freeman III finished high school and went to Prairie View College near Houston. I went to his graduation from college in 2005. At Freeman III's graduation, Brendetta told me she did not know whether she would attend Freeman III's graduation, and I did not thoroughly understand what she meant until later.

In 2003, doctors diagnosed Brendetta with breast cancer. Both sides of the family members were devastated because we knew how close Brendetta and Freeman were.

Brendetta's mother came to Texas to be with them and take her for her chemotherapy treatments. Brendetta seldom complained about her illness because she was strong and did not want any pity parties.

Freeman and Brendetta had a couple who cleaned the house weekly. Friends and neighbors assisted with taking the twins to school and their other activities, including cooking and other chores.

My sister Beatrice and I visited Freeman and Brendetta before she passed away. Early on October 27, 2007, the telephone rang, my sister Beatrice was on the other end, and she told me that Brendetta had expired. Freeman was the first person who came to my mind. I had hip replacement surgery 20 days before her death, but I knew I had to be with Freeman.

Therefore, I called my surgeon and told him that I had a death in the family and needed to fly to Texas. He said it was safe for me to go if I adhered to my restrictions. Beatrice could not go for several days, so I purchased my ticket and left.

I was in Texas two days later. Freeman picked me up from the airport as usual. Immediately, he talked to me about Brendetta's last days. The ambulance took her to the hospital as usual. Freeman III was out of town,even though he was reluctant to go, his mother assured him that she would be all right. Freeman and the girls went to the hospital to visit Brendetta. Freeman said that Brendetta told the girls to remember her advice about young boys.

After they talked for a while, Brendetta's friend took the girls to her home. Freeman and Brendetta's mother continued talking, and she told him she was ready to go home, and that was the last thing she said to him. Freeman was devastated.

Brendetta's mother, relatives, and friends prepared the obituary and repass activities. Relatives and friends from all over the United States attended the service.

Freeman, the children, and other families living without Brendetta were sad and lonely. Mrs. Pruitt stayed in Texas to help with the children for a while. Later, the children lived with a close family friend who babysat them when they were younger.

Between 2009 and 2011, I went to Texas for the twins' graduation from high school and Freeman III's graduation from Prairie View near Huston, Texas, with his Master of Science Degree. I also attended the National Coalition of One Hundred Black Women's Chapter in San Antonio, where Freeman received an award honoring the legend.

Mrs. Pruitt passed away in January 2011 after a brief illness. Her son, Earl Lee Pruitt, who was on dialysis for several years, passed away less than two weeks after his mother. When I learned of his death, I was shocked.

Alana and Jeffery made Freeman a proud grandfather with the birth of Triston K. Jordan-Minor. As of September 20, 2020, Freeman III is unmarried and has no children.

On September 3, 2016, Freeman married Regina Williams, and his family attended the ceremony. They had a home built in Schertz, Texas, close to his previous home in San Antonio. As of September 2022, he still works and is in good health, and we talk and text frequently.

Freeman's brother, Jimmy, has been married twice, and he and his first wife had one son, Jimmy Jr. Jimmy and his second wife have three children and three grandchildren. He is retired from his law enforcement job and currently works part-time.

Freeman's second brother, Gregory, has never been married and has no children.

My niece, Elisia, has been married, and she has one daughter, who is 13 years old. She lives in a suburban area of Chicago, has a bachelor's degree, and is progressive. She and her daughter care for Felisia's son, and the family appreciates her help. May G-d bless her.

My niece, Felisia, the youngest child, has a six-year-old son. She passed away on September 22, 2020, after a brief illness.

End of Bea and her family.

Calvin III

Next is Calvin, my seventh and last brother. He was curious, and hard-headed. To avoid getting in trouble and being punished, he did things I told him. When we lived in White Cloud, Calvin and I were in a shed with a piece of equipment that was attached to a vehicle, and he pushed the equipment into the wall and had to replace it before Papa discovered what happened.

One day we were passing an apple tree loaded with ripe apples. We picked a few of them, then I told Calvin we had enough apples and should leave; however, he decided to get a few more apples. The owner came out and told us it was all right for us to have a few apples, which he gave us, and he took back the rest.

Calvin stayed in White Cloud for several months; then, like Beatrice, he returned to Chicago. He lived with Farroz or Maggie, attended the University of Islam, and worked part-time while Papa, Mama, and I lived in White Cloud. When we moved back to Illinois, Calvin lived with us for a while and worked at various jobs.

Calvin married Emma Johnson, who was one of his high school classmates. They had three daughters, Janet, Lorraine, and Karen. However, they divorced when the children were young, and the children remained with their mother.

Calvin never remarried, but he did have two sons with two different mothers. He lived with one of his son's mothers, Josephine, and her children Renee, Yolanda, Michael, and Jerry, plus their son, Calvin IV, for many years. Josephine passed away after a prolonged illness.

Renee had three daughters, all of whom are grown, and most have children. Yolanda is married and has an articulate 12-year-old daughter. They all love and respect Calvin, whom they call daddy and granddaddy.

Renee was remarkably close to Calvin and treated him like she was his mother. I was also close to Renee. In July 2008, Renee was outside talking to someone and dropped dead immediately. Her children, grandchildren, family members, and friends were devastated by her death.

I asked Yolanda how she addressed my brother, and she said daddy because he took care of her little brother and taught them to be respectful and highly moral. I appreciated her remarks, which made me feel good about my brother because he could have disrespected them.

Josephine was ill for several years, then she passed away.

For many years, Calvin lived with Vivian, my brother Farraz's wife's niece, who had two adult children: a daughter,

Lenora, and a son, Richard. Lenora and Richard each had one son. Lenora lives in Atlanta, Georgia, and frequently travels to Africa.

Richard lived in Chicago and was on dialysis for several years; he passed away about three years ago.

Vivian was caring and like an extended family member. She had emphysema for many years and frequently went to urgent care facilities for treatment. She lived for many years with emphysema; however, she finally succumbed to it.

Presently, Calvin lives with Josephine's oldest daughter, Yolanda, and her family in Chicago. Because all of Josephine's children and grandchildren appreciate Calvin's help raising them. They all welcome him to live with one of them if needed.

You know my siblings, and now it is time to become acquainted with me.

My Adolescent Years

Chapter 5
My Adolescent Life & Community Families

I am Calvin and Georgia Jordan's last child, Delores Daaimah Jardan [1], born at home on August 8, 1935, in Chicago, Illinois, delivered by Sister Martha Ali, my Godmother. While my mother was pregnant with me, she protested sending her children to public school, and the police arrested her. I was a convict before I was born (wow).

My earliest memories, as a child, were having surgery for rickets because my mother lacked sufficient calcium in her diet, and my father did not want me to grow up with bent legs. When the doctor sedated me, I could not breathe; I thought I was suffocating and started fighting for my life. That was an unforgettable experience for me.

However, the operation was successful; I had casts on my legs. When the doctors removed the casts, my legs were straight, and I did not have any problems until later in life.

I started school at the University of Islam when I was eight years old until the police arrested the brothers in 1943. I enjoyed school and learning. When the brothers returned from prison, I went back to school from 1945 until 1946. Then our family moved from Chicago to Michigan.

Before moving to Michigan, I knew several Muslim families whose children were near my age. They are listed below.

Wallace D. and Akbar Muhammad, Children of the Honorable Elijah and Sister Clara Muhammad

When I worked for the Nation of Islam, I saw Wallace occasionally. When he was in his father's presence, he was humble, shy, and good-looking. He married a sister named Shirley, and they had children.

I never thought that anything would happen to the Honorable Elijah Muhammad, but I believed Wallace would replace him, and he did.

Wallace (Imam Warith Deen Muhammad) was an Islamic Scholar who spoke Arabic and thoroughly knew the Holy Quran. His khutbahs were electrifying. When he replaced his father, he gave those who came with him a thorough understanding of Islam. What came to my mind when I heard of his death was *Allah snatched him away from us.* I am still in denial!

Akbar, Wallace D's younger brother, was vivacious. I also saw him occasionally when I worked for the Nation, and we talked about school and education.

Akbar married a beautiful young sister, Harriett, whom I knew, but I am unsure who her parents were. Before moving to Egypt, they lived in a split-level house in Chicago, which I loved. He attended the University of Al Azar and married an Egyptian sister.

Harriett returned to the United States, lived in Los Angeles for a while, then became a journalist for the Muslim newspaper. She brought me a necklace from Egypt, which I still have.

Before I left Chicago, Harriett told me to contact a bank in California to transfer my bank accounts, which I did. I appreciated her assistance.

After returning from Egypt, she remarried and had two daughters. I have not seen her for many years; however, I had the pleasure of having Lottie Muhammad's daughter and the Honorable Elijah Muhammad's granddaughter visit me in May of 2021. She told me that Harriett and her family are well and still living in the United States, which was good news.

Akbar also returned to the United States as a professor at Binghamton University, where he taught African American History. I saw Akbar in the late 1990s at an annual convention in September in Chicago. I was delighted to see him, even though I did not have an opportunity to talk with him because he was on the podium, and I was in the audience. Unfortunately, there was no one around that I knew to take him a note.

The Karim Family

Gloria Karim, daughter of Brother Shelby and Sister Viola Karim, is a former student of the University of Islam, and is still living. She had five older brothers and three older sisters. Gloria speaks and reads Arabic. Her mother was an MGT and GCC captain (Muslim Girls Training and General Civilization) in 1950.

The Shah Family

Joanne's parents were Riza and Henrietta Shah. She had one older brother, two younger brothers, and a younger sister. Beatrice and Joanne remained friends until Joanne passed away some years ago. The Shahs were the same family where Beatrice lived when she left White Cloud, Michigan.

Brother Henry and Sister Idella

Vivian G. Pearl's parents were Brother Henry and Sister Idella. She and I were born in the same year; her birth month is April and mine is August. She is an only child; however, she told me recently that her parents had another child, but she passed away. I thought her parents owned property; however, she said her father was the building's maintenance personnel. The owner of the building was Lorraine Hansberry, a well-known playwright. Vivian's mother was the bookkeeper and kept the records for the property.

Vivian attended the University of Islam and graduated. She married when she was eighteen, and she and her husband had seven children: four daughters, and three sons. Her youngest daughter passed away in 2010.

When I returned to Chicago in 1955, Vivian had been married for two years and had one child; therefore, we did not frequently see each other because she was busy with her family.

I moved to California in 1960 and did not see Vivian often when I was in Chicago, until her children were older. However, when I visited my family or attended the annual Islamic conventions, we saw each other and went shopping at our favorite store, Carso, in the Cicero Mall. Occasionally, we went to the convention together. She enjoys sewing and is an excellent seamstress.

Brother Carl and Sister Maggie's Family

Darnell's parents were Brother Carl and Sister Maggie who became members of the Nation of Islam after Fard Muhammad left Chicago. He had one older brother and two younger siblings,

49

a sister, Rosaland, and Carl Jr. Years later, Brother Carl and Sister Maggie had another child. Rosaland and I were friends. She married young, and she and her husband had six children.

Although Brother Carl and Sister Maggie had not been members of the Nation of Islam for long before the brothers went to jail, he also went. However, Sister Maggie let their children remain in the school, which I admired.

Darnell, Rosaland, Gloria Karim, and other students who attended the University of Islam learned Arabic from an Egyptian couple whom the Honorable Elijah Muhammad hired. Darnell is exceptionally proficient in Arabic, authors a weekly article in the Muslim Journal, and is also an Imam. Additionally, I memorized some of the surahs in part 30 from his Quranic tapes. Darnell and Gloria Karim married in 1959 and have six children and grandchildren.

I see Darnell and Gloria occasionally at Islamic Events. For example, I saw them at a conference in Berkeley, CA, on October 26-27, 2018. Darnell is the last member of his family, and Gloria and her oldest sister, Lucille, and one brother are the three remaining members of the Karim Family. May Allah bless them.

The Eskridge Family

Eskridge had five sons and four daughters. One of those children was my life-long friend, Emma (Stephanie); we met at a youthful age.

She graduated from the University of Islam in 1955, and she was proficient in Arabic. Emma's mother passed away in childbirth with her last child. Since Emma was the oldest female child in the household, she had to assume responsibility for household chores with her paternal grandmother, and Emma was not her favorite grandchild.

Emma was talented, an excellent seamstress, and a cook. She could look at an item, then go home and make that same garment. So, we took a sewing class together; she paid for the course, and I bartered for mine by typing for two hours one evening before the class.

Emma married John Anthony, who adored her; they had two sons. They moved to Los Angeles, California, purchased a home, and had another son some years later.

She changed her name to Stephanie, attended West Los Angeles College, earned an A.A. degree in accounting and worked for LAUSD. Then she worked for the State of California as an Administrative Assistant.

John Anthony and Stephanie divorced, and when I learned of their divorce, I was dismayed because he adored her. Several years after they divorced, Stephanie remarried John W. Blake. She always called him Blake, and then I realized why, because her first spouse's name was also John.

I am not sure of the year, but John Anthony passed away. Since he was the father of their sons, Stephanie attended the funeral; I also went to the service since she was my friend and for moral support if she needed it.

Stephanie and John Blake bought a house in Riverside, California, and Stephanie lavishly decorated the house. Since I lived in Los Angeles, California Stephanie and I talked and visited each other periodically. In addition, we attended a health class in a health food store on Wednesday evenings, which was informative.

John Blake passed away in 2002, and Stephanie expired in January 2009. I miss her.

Brother Joseph 5X and Sister Elsie's Family

Lorraine's parents, Brother Joseph 5X, his wife Sister Elsie, and their other children Lawrence and Geraldine, became members of the Nation of Islam in the 1950s when I lived in Hopkins Parks, Illinois. Her mother was an MGT and GCC Captain in the 1950s. Vivian told me that she was a caring person.

My good friend Lorraine was compassionate, caring, kind, and pleasant. She had a nursery in her home, and my nephew, Freeman, was one of her students.

We were on a flight from Chicago with a group of people to a city to hear the Honorable Elijah Muhammad speak. Lorraine and I sat together, and she talked about many topics, including her desire to marry. I was glad that we sat together to relieve some of her frustration.

Wallace and Lorraine married and had a daughter. When Wallace became Imam W. Deen Muhammad, his grown daughter became one of his secretaries.

I saw Lorraine at a Labor Day Weekend Convention in Chicago before 2008, caring for her grandson and assisting her daughter, who had a booth. I believe Lorraine lives in Atlanta with her daughter; however, I am unsure. I wish her the best.

Other Family Members of the Honorable Elijah Muhammad

The Honorable Elijah Muhammad's father, his Mother Marie, and his sister, Sister Anna, were also pioneers. The

Honorable Elijah Muhammad and his father was the same complexion; however, his father was slightly larger than he.

Chapter 6
Pioneers I Knew

When I was young, I knew many pioneers in Chicago who were members of the Nation of Islam. Some of them are below.

Sister Martha Ali and Her Daughter

Sister Martha Ali was my godmother and an MGT and GCC Captain in 1950. She also designed the sisters' first uniform. Her daughter, Sister Josephine Ali, was the Nation's Secretary.

Brother Marcella Jordan, not my father, was a captain. He was a stately brother, and I do not believe he was ever married.

Brother Ephram Bahar married Sister Tennessee, an MGT and GCC Captain. I do not recall them having any children.

Sister Lady B and family

Rarely do you see a biological family accepting the same religion as this one. This family had six sisters and three brothers: Sister Lady Bee, Sister Ruby, Sisters Margaret, Annie, Lillie, Susie, and Brothers Alvin, Harvey, and Casey. All the sisters lived together on the west side of Chicago in a two-story house on Green Street, except Sister Susie. Sister Susie lived alone, and I do not recall her marrying; she had no children.

Sister Lady Bea lived in California for five or more years; she returned to Chicago and is now deceased.

All the sisters were excellent cooks, and they had an open-house policy. During Savior's Day time, many people from out of the state visited them. Their home was a warm and enjoyable place to go.

Sister Queenie, aka Malika Omar, and Her Grandson

Sister Queenie was an attractive and personable woman who became a member of the Nation of Islam in 1946 in Cincinnati, Ohio. She had two adult daughters, a younger son, Robert, and at least two grandsons that she raised, who were close to her son. They moved to Chicago in 1955.

Before moving to Chicago in 1955, she was Sister Queenie. After 1975, she was Malika Omar, and her grandson Abraham attended the Nation of Islam annual February convention. Before the convention began, some former and current students practiced the call to prayer. Among the students were Wallace Muhammad, Darnell, Akbar Muhammad, and Akbar's nephew, Hassan. Abraham said their performance electrified him. As a result, his grandmother decided to move to Chicago so her son and grandsons could attend the University of Islam.

Abraham attended the University of Islam from 12 to 17, graduated high school, and continued. He had many positions in the Nation of Islam, including a lieutenant. Abraham was Wallace D. Muhammad's security guard and continued when Imam Muhammad became the Nation of Islam's leader. Abraham gained so much knowledge from traveling with Imam Warith Deen Mohammed that he became well-qualified to teach the religion. In 1976, there was a vacancy for an Imam in Atlanta, Georgia. Imam Muhammad sent Imam Abraham to replace the previous Imam. He married and had several children. Later, he became a Shaykh.

I saw Shaykh Abraham at an event in California; I also saw him in 2009 when I visited Atlanta, Georgia.

Shaykh Abraham returned to Allah in 2016. May Allah grant him the highest place in Paradise for dedicating his entire adult life to the Muslim Community. His grandmother passed away in 2020. May Allah also accept her honorable deeds and grant her Paradise.

Chapter 7
Illinois

As previously stated, we lived in White Cloud, Michigan, a Caucasian area. Our father did not let us attend school; therefore, when we moved to Illinois, I enrolled myself and my brother Calvin in the community's one-room elementary school. I was jubilant to be with other people my age. Whenever the teacher asked who wanted to go to the board to do mathematics problems, I raised my hand. I loved mathematics as well as all the other subjects we had. However, I did not want my classmates to think I was a showoff; I allowed the other students to go to the board.

I also socialized with some of my classmates. One of my classmates invited me to a picnic on Sunday after church. I arrived early and entered the church, which was quite different from my previous religious services. When the service ended, the members started running around the church, which was their way of praising G-d. I learned something new.

Secondary School

Most of us who graduated from elementary school, in the rural area we lived in, attended Momence Community High School. Momence Community High School was different and more extensive than the one-room school we graduated from, with many more departments and students. All the staff were

Caucasian. The elementary school students were primarily African Americans living in St. Anne's rural area. Most of the Caucasian students lived in the town of Momence; one of their families owned the local morgue.

I did not pass the proficiency tests; therefore, I took algebra in my sophomore year and received an "A" in the class. I should have continued with mathematics, but there was only one math teacher, whom I did not care for. I realize that I only hurt myself.

School counselors gave most minority students industrial art programs, and others had academic programs. One of my Afro-American friends, Annette Johnson, who was very bright, got a scholarship to college. I had the pleasure of seeing and having lunch with Annette one summer in Chicago, and it was an enjoyable afternoon. We have also talked on the telephone since I saw her.

How I Spent My Summer Vacations

Some summers, I worked in fields for farmers near where I lived. Working on large acres of land, sitting, or bending to cut vegetables was hard. I also worked in Chicago during my school vacation to purchase my school clothing. Since my sister, Geneva, loved to shop, especially at boutique stores, she took me shopping. Of course, I could not pay cash for the items; therefore, I put them on layaway and finished paying for them before returning to school. I worked at a museum one summer, cleaning tables and washing dishes.

During some summer vacations, I babysat for my sister, Beatrice, and cousin Edward, and his wife, Doris, who were like an older brother and sister. I also babysat one of their neighbors' children, saving them some money. Additionally, that was more money for me to purchase my clothes. I enjoyed babysitting at that complex because there was a pool, and on hot days, we put our feet in the swimming pool while we relaxed and ate Good Humor ice cream bars.

I also babysat for Charlotte and Emanual Muhammad, the Honorable Elijah Muhammad's children, when they lived in Muhammad's previous home on Michigan Avenue. Charlotte was personable and a friend of my sisters, Geneva, and Beatrice. She had a sister, Dorothy; their parents were Brother Alfonso and Sister Susie.

Night Life. Returned to Chicago

After graduating from high school in 1955, I went back to Chicago to live with my sister Beatrice. In August 1955, Emmitt Till, a 14-year-old African American child, was brutally murdered when a Caucasian female alleged that he flirted with her. I went to the mortuary for the open casket viewing. His face resembled old paper that had been in a closet for years. I could only think that little had changed.

I started looking for employment. I worked on production lines in mail-order stores, with the last hired-first fired policy, which was not to my liking. I did that for several years, and then it got tiring.

I went to dancing halls and clubs on weekends with friends and acquaintances. There was a beautiful ballroom in the neighborhood where I lived. For many years it was exclusively for Caucasians. After most Caucasians moved from the community, the Afro-Americans started attending the facility. It sounded like raindrops falling from the sky when you walked on the floor. I enjoyed that place.

Occasionally, well-known musicians performed there; sometimes, they would pull off their neckties and shirts and throw them to the audience. When that occurred, to avoid being trampled by screaming females trying to get a piece of a sweaty shirt or tie, I moved away from the stage.

Went Back to the Temple and Became Active

Partying on the weekends was not as exciting as it appeared. My childhood lifestyle as a member of the Nation of Islam was better for me; therefore, I decided that New Year's Eve, 1957, would be the last one for that lifestyle, and I returned to the Temple and became active.

I traveled with believers to various cities where the Honorable Elijah Muhammad spoke. I always wanted to visit New York and California, so when the Honorable Elijah Muhammad spoke in New York I went. New York was a disappointment to me. Besides being congested, Harlem was muggy, and dirty. The buildings were too close together or had no space between them at all, and I wondered how the people who lived there breathed.

Minister Malcolm X was the head minister. He was charismatic, the crowd was large and triumphant, and everyone enjoyed the meeting.

I also traveled to Washington, D.C. with the mother of my friend Vivian , for one of the Honorable Elijah Muhammad's speeches. The trips were spiritually enlightening, and we also met sisters from other parts of the United States.

The temple in Chicago on 54th and Greenwood had an apartment downstairs, where believers from out of town stayed for one or two nights. One evening I received a call from an official asking me whether I could spend the night in the apartment with Sister Betty, who married Minister Malcolm, so she would not be alone. I agreed. When I married, she gave me a set of beautiful white and lilac towels, and I am sure I still have at least one towel. May Allah bless her and grant her Paradise.

Ramadan

We started preparing for Savior's Day at the beginning of the new year. The committee requested members to donate $100.00. I did domestic work for Caucasians on the North Side of Chicago to earn extra money for my donation. I felt good when I paid my $100.00.

Additionally, the drill team was practicing for their annual performance, and I wanted to participate; therefore, I asked Captain Lottie Muhammad whether I could join the team. She said, "yes," and I began practicing. Gloria Karim was the drill team captain; she was an excellent captain, and we worked hard. We also sang a song, *Let us hear the Call of Allah, La ilaha illAllah Muhammadur Rasulullah.*

The seamstress made the uniforms for the drill team members. However, I knew how to sew and made my own uniform. Unfortunately, when we dressed to drill, Sister Captain told me that my material was not as heavy as the other sisters; hence, I did not perform with the team. I was disappointed, but life went on.

Shortly after that, Sister Captain made me her first lieutenant. I taught classes in the MGT & GCC, stood post, and assisted sisters in learning lessons, the problem book, and other needed activities. But discipline was not one of my strong skills.

I was a lieutenant for a while; then, I started working for the Nation of Islam, not your typical 8:00 am to 4:00 pm job. Since Sister Captain was not pleased with my weak disciplining skills, she was not sad when I left. However, we remained friends after I moved from Chicago and went back to visit; she invited me to her home, and I spent an enjoyable afternoon with her.

Sister Captain said something at the MGT class that left an indelible impression on me; she remarked, "a man could fall, get stained, pick himself up, brush himself off, and continue. However, the stain remains if a woman falls and becomes stained."

Chapter 8
Working for The Nation of Islam

I got tired of being the last one hired and the first fired; hence, I decided to work for the Nation of Islam. I called the Honorable Elijah Muhammad to see whether he needed any help, and he said he did. So I went for the interview, and he hired me. Since I lived in the neighborhood, I could walk to work during the spring and summer, but not the winter months.

Three or four sisters were working there when I started. Our working hours were from 10:00 am until we finished, or someone could take us home. Mondays were usually long days because the Honorable Elijah Muhammad authored an article in a newspaper that he mailed on Mondays. After he had drafted the article, he gave it to the secretary to type. When she finished typing the article, she returned the paper to him. If he approved the report, we went home. But, if he returned the item to the secretary, she made the corrections until he accepted the write-up. Then, we went home.

Some of my duties were to check letters from individuals interested in becoming members of the Nation of Islam.

Before 1975, membership in the Nation of Islam required several steps. For example, when I started working in 1958, a person who wanted to become a member of the Nation of Islam wrote a letter declaring his intention. The letter was not challenging to write, but penmanship was crucial. Many people had to write the letter several times and were not discouraged.

Once the letter passed, the person started attending special classes on Monday, FOI for the men and MGT and GCC for the women on Thursday, where they learned English Lesson No. C1, which I believe was a chronology of Fard Muhammad's past. We had a law that Sister Captain read at each meeting. I do not recall all the content, but I remember that part that said, "do not commit adultery; go not near it." The religion of Islam emphasized high morals.

The Honorable Elijah Muhammad frequently had guests, ministers from the United States, and dignitaries from other countries; therefore, the secretaries rotated in serving dinner. Minister Louis Farrakhan, the minister of the Temple in Boston, Massachusetts, was also a guest of the Honorable Elijah Muhammad. He addressed the Honorable Elijah Muhammad as "Dear Holy Apostle." Minister Farrakhan was a former Calypso Singer and had a song called "The White Man's Heaven is the Black Man's Hell."

If the secretaries were not terribly busy, we had the opportunity to sit at the table while the Honorable Elijah Muhammad answered his guests' questions or explained something to them. Those conversations were very enlightening. Also, the secretaries could put faces to the names of the ministers with whom they corresponded.

When she finished serving dinner, she assisted the cook in washing the dishes and cleaning the kitchen.

I remember two of the cooks, Sister Frances, who worked for a long time, and Sister Pearl, for whom I was a babysitter as a teenager. She was warm, kind, and caring, and did not let minor things bother her. She would say, "don't worry about that," "it is not important," and "forget it."

She had four daughters and one older son. Because I admired her, I helped her comb their hair and press their dresses; many of which she made because she was an excellent seamstress. I am sure she made clothes for me.

Sister Pearl and her husband passed away in an automobile accident in the 1970s, while returning home from visiting relatives.

When the Honorable Elijah Muhammad spoke in other Midwest cities, Detroit, Michigan; Cleveland, Ohio; some secretaries went with him, Sister Clara Muhammad, and other family members usually caravanned. When he visited cities in the East, we flew.

The Honorable Elijah Muhammad visited a city, I believe, on the East Coast with a large auditorium filled with people. Sitting there, I wondered whether the Honorable Elijah Muhammad would use the term "devils;" and he did. WOW! Mike Wallace, the late reporter from *60 Minutes*, called the Honorable Elijah Muhammad's speech "The Hate that Hate Produced."

When we attended meetings out of town, the secretaries sat in the front; however, I did not like being in the spotlight. Therefore, I asked a sister in charge of security whether she needed any assistance since they welcomed help from Temple #2 sisters.

May Allah bless her for her services to the Nation of Islam and grant her Paradise.

Minister Malcolm

I met Minister Malcolm while working as a secretary and serving dinner at the Honorable Elijah Muhammad's house. He took his position as spokesperson for the Honorable Elijah Muhammad seriously. Otherwise, he was personable.

Someone told him I was getting married and moving to California. He was pleased because the brother was from Boston, and Minister Malcolm knew him. Additionally, I visited Ronald's sister, Bea, in South Carolina in July 2021, and she told me that she knew Minister Malcolm when he was young and worked at the soda counter in a drug store she frequented. Also, one of Minister Malcolm's male cousins married a female Stokes. So that accounted for the close relationship between Minister Malcolm and my husband Ronald.

Minister Malcolm told me California was beautiful and I would like the weather because it only rained in the winter months.

Looking for Changes in my Life

Since I was almost twenty-five, several of my friends were already married and had children, so I started thinking about marriage myself.

Uncle Leland's son, Edward, introduced me to Frank Moe, Edward's mother's nephew's stepson. He was a handsome young man who lived in East Saint Louis, Illinois. After we met, Frank went to the Army, and we corresponded while he was away. When he returned home from the Army, he came by to see me one evening, and he said that we had known each other long enough to "play married." I disagreed since I feared my Lord and respected myself. Additionally, how could I not respect myself since the captain read the law every Thursday at MGT, stating fornication and adultery were forbidden? Of course, that was the end of our friendship.

Frank's brother came to Chicago; he stopped by the house and told me that Frank had married. I was sad, but life continued.

I admired Darnell Karim's oldest brother, Leroy, but he thought of me as Calvin's little sister, although I was only about two years younger than him. There was a shortage of eligible brothers my age because most were already married. I saw Darnell years later and asked him, "How is your brother?" He told me that Leroy never got married, and his preference was not African American women.

The Savior's Day season was an occasion to meet eligible brothers, since some ministers and believers came to Chicago early and met at the Savior's Day meeting location. During the late 1950s, there was one young eligible minister in Hartford, Connecticut, and one in Buffalo, New York. The Minister from Hartford, Connecticut was interested in a sister who lived in Chicago that I knew, but nothing materialized from that meeting, nor did anything materialize from the minister from Buffalo.

Met an East Coast Brother

On Savior's Day, 1960, I went to the facility for the February 26 meeting to listen to some speakers. It was at this meeting that I met Ronald Townson Stokes. After the meeting, he came to where I was sitting, spoke to me, and introduced himself. It was then I realized we lived in the same apartment building owned by a Muslim couple, Sister Louise, and her husband, Brother Arthur. I shared an apartment with a sister in that building, and Ronald shared an apartment with a brother.

We had a brief conversation, then we departed. Ronald was handsome, articulate, and well-built, and I hoped that I would see him again; and I did.

Because my working hours were irregular, I seldom saw Ronald during the week; however, we saw each other on weekends and started learning about each other.

He was born and raised in Roxbury, Massachusetts, where his parents and siblings lived. He attended primary school, an all-boys secondary school, and pharmaceutical classes in Massachusetts. He served in the Korean war. Before coming to Chicago, he and his sister's ten-year-old son spent a year in California. What a responsible person and a trusting sister.

When I visited his sister in 2021, she told me Ronald attended meetings with the Nation of Islam before they had a Temple.

Ronald was the youngest of his siblings; he had an older brother and a sister. His brother was married and had two children. His brother's wife was a member of the Nation of Islam, and she introduced Ronald to the Nation. His sister, Bea, had four children; three sons, and one daughter. I do not remember Ronald's father's occupation, but he worked on his job for many years. His mother was and had been a seamstress for a long time.

Ronald's roommate in Chicago had an automobile, and sometimes on hot evenings, the three of us would ride around the city or go to a drive-thru McDonald's in Indiana, which was close to where we lived, and purchase shakes. That was enjoyable.

Ronald went home annually to help his father maintain their properties. They had a large apartment building in Roxbury with three or four floors where the family and tenants lived. They also had a summer home in Maine. While he was there, Ronald sent me a postcard and a letter. The letter stated he told his family he had met a sister and intended to ask her to marry him when he returned to Chicago.

When Ronald returned from Roxbury in May 1960, he started planning our marriage and moving to California; therefore, we did not rent an apartment. I contacted my tailor and had my dress made.

Ronald lived in California before he came to Chicago, and he loved it and wanted to live there. He knew several reliable brothers in California, Brother Randolph, and Brother Willie, who found us an apartment near the temple.

Ronnie made the airline reservations early since we were going to leave Chicago after the wedding. Close to the wedding date, I sent some of my clothes to Sister Lady Bea, who had relocated from Chicago to California.

I looked forward to meeting Ronald's family, and I was not disappointed. They were friendly, and we quickly started a conversation as though we were old friends.

Mrs. Stokes sent me several other items. I still have the lingerie set in a container. Mr. Stokes was quiet.

Married Life

Chapter 9
Married Ronald Townsend Stokes and Moved to Los Angeles

T he wedding was at my Sister Geneva's house because we did not expect a large crowd. Ronald's parents, sister, and children came from Boston for the wedding. Of course, my parents, several of my siblings, and cousins attended the wedding.

After giving our families farewell hugs, kisses, and wishes for good health and a safe return to Ronnie's family, a friend took us to the airport, and we were on our way to California.

Of course, we were exhausted and slept most of the flight to California. Brothers Randolph and Willie picked us up when we arrived at the airport. After introductions and greetings, they took us to our beautiful, new upstairs single apartment. Ronnie drove to the brother's home so he could use the car the next day. When he returned, we went to bed and had a fulfilling night for which we waited for months and then slept.

My 20-Months with Ronald

We visited Ronnie's friends, who he previously knew when he lived in Los Angeles. Among them were Captain Edward and his family. Captain Edward was a Juvenile Counselor for the City of Los Angeles. They had an older daughter and son, and after a few years, they had another daughter.

Deanne, Captain Edward 2X and his wife, Jean's youngest daughter, was my student at the Sister Clara Muhammad School in 1970. Deanne is married and has two daughters and one grandson.

I talked to her recently, and she invited me to her home for the weekend. However, since Covid set in, I have not been able to visit her. In sha Allah, I will be able to visit soon.

We also visited one of Ronald's cousins during our first month in Los Angeles, who lived in Compton. Many Afro-Americans had beautiful homes in Compton in the 1960s. Unfortunately, Ronald's cousin's son passed away in the Korean war.

He took me to one of his favorite ice cream parlors and purchased ice cream. His sister told me that he loved ice cream and watermelon.

Since we did not have any food in the apartment, we went out for dinner and bought some food and other items from the grocery market. Ronald had already told me that his mother cooked potato salad and macaroni and cheese for dinner every Sunday; he did not need more of those foods.

He also told me to take the bed sheets to the Chinese laundry and, at night, fold the bedspread and put it at the end of the bed. Ronnie was not a dominating person; but wanted me to know his likes and dislikes, and that was what I did, and we were both pleased. Then, since he enjoyed being active in the Temple, he became secretary.

I cooked, cleaned, and washed the clothes; Ronald took and picked up the linen and laundry and paid the bills. He was very caring, kind, and considerate, and helped me with some household chores.

We rested, saw more of his old friends, and did some sightseeing for several weeks; then we started looking for employment.

We had already talked about looking for jobs before we left Chicago. Also, a sister who had recently moved to Chicago from California gave me some suggestions.

Government jobs are usually more secure than private employment, and government jobs are abundant.

Both of us applied to the County of Los Angeles for jobs, and Ronald got a job at the purchasing department on Soto. The Department of Public Services (DPSS) employed me as a beginner clerk-typist, and I was professionally qualified for that position.

DPSS was a huge two-floor building located on Adams and Grand close to downtown Los Angeles, providing social services for needy people. Social workers, supervisors, and clerical employees assisted the public. Intake workers initiated the procedure to determine the individual's needs; then, the social worker decided what services would be provided.

We worked and attended the Temple on Wednesday and Friday evenings and Sunday afternoons. Ronald attended the FOI meeting on Monday, and I went to the MGT meeting on Thursday evening. Those meetings were classes for members of The Nation of Islam.

A disturbing incident occurred while living on West 51st Street. A brother, whom Ronald knew, decapitated his wife because she would not become a member of the Nation of Islam. I never encountered such a horrific act. Some brothers divorced their wives.

A brother in Los Angeles had a food market with a meat case, but he did not sell meat, so Ronald rented the area, and we sold kosher chicken on the weekends.

We moved to a larger apartment on 56th and Broadway at the end of the block from Temple #27; it was very convenient. One night, shortly after moving there, we went out with a brother and his wife, and someone broke into our apartment. When we returned and Ronald saw what happened, he said he should go to the next-door neighbors to ask whether they saw anyone. I told him that I did not believe that was a promising idea. I thought the person who broke into the apartment knew he was the secretary. They knew we weren't home and that there was probably some money in the house, so forget about asking the neighbors anything.

Minister Malcolm visited Los Angeles, and while he was there, he and a young brother in Los Angeles, Norman, had dinner with us. Whenever Norman aka Yusuf saw me, he reminded me that our home was the first Muslim home where he had dinner. Norman always had a smile on his face.

When Yusuf became an adult, he married and he and his wife moved to Atlanta, Georgia, where they raised their family. Their children have been quite successful, including a doctor and a dentist.

First Child

At the end of seven months of marriage, we learned that we would be parents—what a happy occasion because Ronnie loved children. He used to run his fingers through a little boy's hair at the Temple, and the child told his dad, and his dad said it was okay.

I needed to find a female obstetrician. I am sure I called Captain Edward's wife, Jean, and she found me exactly what I needed. She referred me to an Afro-American female obstetrician in, Watts, California, who was precisely what I needed. She was my prenatal and postnatal physician. My pregnancy was uneventful. I did not have any morning sickness; however, Ronald had evening sickness; I felt sorry for him because he had a low tolerance for pain.

Sister JoAnn, whom I still know, had recently given birth. She offered me some maternity clothes, which I accepted.

Jean and I talked frequently. She was a paralegal and worked for an attorney in Watts, California, and recommended I learn legal terms, to replace her if she needed a substitute. I replaced her once while I was on parental leave.

Several sisters including Sister Captain Mamie, and Sisters Mary and Marie gave me a baby shower and provided essential items. In addition, someone brought food for the occasion.

I went into labor on a Friday night when Ronald was at the Temple. He was the secretary and never came home until he calculated and secured the funds. When he came home, I told him that I was in labor. However, since the pain was not consistent, we waited until the following day before going to the hospital.

Ronald took me to the hospital and left. Remember, he could not tolerate pain for himself or others; besides, he had to go to the market where we had a concession. I assumed he was talking to his sister, who had a son two months earlier in October, to ensure everything was all right with me.

I was in labor all day; I called on my mother in Illinois when the pain intensified. The doctor mentioned C-Section, and I said no.

The baby, a healthy six-pound plus girl, arrived, then Ronald finally came. A sister, whom I knew from Chicago, visited me earlier in the year and told me she recently had a daughter named Saudia. So, I told her if I *had* a girl, I would call her Saudia Bernice since Bernice is her paternal Grandmother's name.

After I went home, my mother came to visit and help us with the baby and other household chores. I was pleasantly surprised to see her and welcomed her help. Mama, knowing what to do, took over. She prepared delicious bean soup, brown rice, and rolls. We ate well while she was there; however, some good things ended; Mama left, and we took over. Mama gained one more granddaughter; however, two weeks after returning home, she lost her son, Leon.

The baby slept well; she only woke up once or twice during the night. After I breastfed her, changed her if needed, and put her back in the crib, she went back to sleep for the remainder of the night. Good baby.

Ronnie bought a 1962 new Volkswagen, and he and Brothers Randolph and William drove to Chicago for Saviors Day. They had a safe arrival and return. My baby and I spent the nights with Brother Randolph's wife, Maria, and her baby; we stayed home during the day.

Ronnie's parents gave him a down payment for a house, and he started looking. Unfortunately, my family leave ended; therefore, I started looking for a babysitter. I do not know who I selected, but I did find a babysitter, and Ronnie found a two-bedroom home with a sunken front room, dining room, kitchen, breakfast nook, bathroom, and a half in the Leimert Park section of Los Angeles for $18,000. The house was lovely; the neighborhood was changing. Ronnie said we would stay there for several years and then move to View Park or Baldwin Hills.

I returned to work in March of 1962. We moved to our new home on April 1, 1962. Ronnie bought all the house furniture, which was beautiful, and I still have the bedroom dresser.

When Ronald came home one evening, he found the front door unlocked. He was genuinely concerned and told me to be sure to lock the door for our safety. He was so caring; after that, I made certain to lock the door.

Ronnie called his mother a week or two before April 27, 1962. When I visited Mrs. Stokes in Boston, she told me that during their conversation, he said, "Mama, if I do not see you again." She said that she immediately gave the telephone to her daughter. After that, she did not see him again.

After dinner, Friday, April 27, 1962, Ronnie, Saudia, and I went to the Temple. Ronnie completed his secretarial duties and heard some disturbance outside the Temple. He told me to wait inside while he went to see what was happening outside. Brother Earl, who lived near the Temple, came into the temple, and advised the sisters to go over to his house with his wife, and we did. I recently learned from Brother Troy that after the sisters left, the police came inside the Temple and continued shooting the interior of the building and beating the brothers savagely.

Shortly after we arrived at Brother Earl's house, several brothers came to pick me up; they said I needed to go to the County hospital. He took another sister with us. I do not remember anyone telling me why, nor where I was going, and I do not remember asking them. They took us to admissions when we arrived, where several police officers were waiting. One police officer asked, "Who is Mrs. Stokes?" I said, "I am Mrs. Stokes." He said, "Your husband is dead." The officer recommended that I stay at the hospital for the night, and I told him, "No," and I told the group, "Let's go," and we left. I refused to give them any satisfaction by becoming emotional.

The brothers took me to Sister Captain Mamie's house. On the way back from the hospital, I could only think about how I would tell Ronald's parents that he was dead. But thank G-d; I did not have to; they located me. I do not recall what I said to them. I am sure that they told me they were on their way because they arrived several days later. My mother and sister, Beatrice, came from Chicago.

The next day, several sisters took me home. The house felt so cold. As I entered the house, I started crying when I realized Ronald would never walk through that door again. The sisters put away items Ronald left in the bath and bedroom to avoid my seeing them. I got my baby, and some sisters stayed with me until my family members arrived.

Brother Arthur and Minister Henry from Long Beach helped with the funeral arrangements. Minister Malcolm conducted the funeral, which I scarcely remember. I needed to remember to set the *theme* for this service and remain calm and peaceful. Out of compassion, I did not believe I had the right to become emotional, even though I had lost Ronald, my soul mate, after twenty short months of marriage. Still, his parents and family had him for almost 29 years, and they were peaceful.

After the ceremony, a newspaper reporter came toward me, but Minister Malcolm told him, "Do not get in her face," and he left. That is all I remember about the funeral.

After the funeral, I had to decide about our baby, Saudia. Ronald's sister, Beatrice, thought it would be too difficult for me to care for a young baby after the trauma of Ronald's death. She believed it would be better for the family to take Saudia back to Boston. So, when they departed for Boston, Saudia went with them. I was lonely, but it was better for the baby and me. The Stokes, my mother and sister returned home.

Ronald was peaceful, kind, caring, and considerate. All the time I knew him, he never raised his voice at me. It was difficult for me to imagine how we would live without him, but fifty-nine+ years later, we are still here with the help of Allah and prayer, patience, and perseverance .

Various sisters stayed with me until Captain Mamie and Captain Edward selected Brother Randolph and his family to live with me. That was an excellent choice because Ronnie and Brother Randolph were friends who had known each other for about four years. Additionally, they had a daughter one year older than Saudia and would be a companion for Saudia when she returned from Boston. Brother Randolph and his family stayed until my sister Geneva came a year later, then they moved. However, I stayed connected with them and saw them frequently.

Adjusting to Life Without Ronald

About three weeks after Ronald's death, I returned to work. My supervisors and co-workers offered their condolences and were cordial. An employee who worked in the building did not know Ronald Stokes was my late husband. I told her about the incident on April 27, and she related it to her Pastor, who advised her not to ride nor associate with me. I was not upset with her decision. Occasionally, when I walked in the halls, people would tap other people to let them know who I was.

I missed Ronnie very much, and sometimes I needed to cry. Some of the ladies' restrooms had an additional room with small beds; I brought clean sheets to work to lie down and weep when needed.

Even though I was grieving, my work performance did not decrease because I was a proficient typist and enjoyed my job.

However, by August 1962, I needed a change; I had to see my baby. So I went to Mrs. Wilson, the Head Clerical Supervisor, and asked for three weeks off, which she readily gave me. So, I went to Boston to see Saudia and the Stokes family. I was delighted to see all of them, but seeing Mr. Stokes was painful because I could see the grief on his face, and I wanted to remain composed. I imagine that Mrs. Stokes was also grieving, but she was a cheerful person who did not show grief.

Saudia was growing and doing well; I hugged and kissed her. I was also grateful to my sister-in-law for being considerate by keeping Saudia since she had a ten-month-old son and three pre-teens.

That was the first time I had been to Boston; I could not help but think how much joy this trip would be if Ronnie were here; nevertheless, I had an enjoyable time.

We went to the Stokes' summer home in Maine for several days, and to Old Orchard, Maine, near a beach, where we purchased fresh, delicious saltwater taffy in various flavors. Some merchants sold souvenirs, beachwear, and a variety of items. Mrs. Stokes occasionally sent me saltwater taffy. We also went shopping downtown at Filene's, a department store predominantly in the Mid-England States in the 1960s, one of

Bea's and her mother's favorite stores. I liked shopping in the store also.

The Trial

Then the trial started. Attorney Loren Miller was the defense attorney. In his opening statement, he said this tragedy had left Ronald Stokes' wife a widow and his baby an orphan.

The trial for the brothers involved in their unjustified shooting was short, and, of course, they were found guilty and served time. But, after thirty-five minutes of deliberation, justification was the verdict. Is the shooting of a person with his hands above his head justifiable?

The murderer of my husband and the father of my four-month-old daughter said, "I saw this male Negro coming towards me with his hands in the air, and I thought he was going to choke me." I left the court. I never returned because I knew that I could not sit in that court peacefully and listen to them lie about my husband, whom I knew was a kind, gentle, compassionate, clean-cut, respectful individual with no criminal record.

Besides, Ronald was dead, and William Rogers never walked again. The police shot William Rogers' brother, Robert, multiple times while protecting his brother. Robert was visiting William from Philadelphia, on his way to the airport returning home, and not even a member of the Nation of Islam. Many people were scared for their lives, and I did not want to add to that number.

Chapter 10
Expanding My Social Group. New and Old Members.

In the 1960s I started associating with members Ronald and I had previously met, along with new members as well. These are some of the prominent members.

Imam Haroon

Ronald and I met Imam Haroon Abdullah, formerly Minister Henry Battle, of Long Beach when we moved to Los Angeles. He and his wife had been followers of the Nation of Islam since 1959, after hearing the Honorable Elijah Muhammad speak in California.

Before becoming members of the Nation of Islam, Mr. Battle and his wife were active church members. He passionately believed in the Nation of Islam's message of doing for himself. He became involved in Southern and Northern California and nearby areas using Muhammad Speaks Newspaper and the Pittsburg Courier. He became a Minister and opened two temples, one in Watts in 1967 and one on the Westside of Los Angeles in 1969.

In 1972, he became the minister in Long Beach's storefront site with approximately twenty believers. By 1975, Long Beach Temple #42 had grown to over three hundred believers, who changed their names, a Masjid, and an utterly Islamic home for

Muslims from many countries. Imam Haroon attributes much of his success to the Honorable Elijah Muhammad and Imam W. Deen Muhammad.

Imam Haroon Abdullah was pleasant. When I saw him, he greeted me warmly, and we chatted briefly, then we moved on. It was easy to talk with him about my issues. He was humorous when talking about his daughter and grandsons. In one of his lectures regarding Christmas, he told his daughter that the gifts were from him and not Santa Clause. His daughter had to remind him that his three active grandsons were ordinary boys who would not hurt themselves.

In his nineties, Imam Haroon became ill and spent some time in a convalescent facility. He passed away in January of 2018. May Allah accept all the work he did to advance Al Islam and grant him Paradise.

Imam Haroon's wife, Sister Luella Zubaidah, was friendly, quiet, and supportive of her husband. She loved her daughter and grandsons. The masjid had an annual function for the sisters during May; however, the brothers also came. We had a variety of foods, entertainment, and gifts. I looked forward to that event, but when Sister Louella could not continue the May event, the other sisters picked it up and continued.

Sister Louella had a sharp memory. I went to see her in a convalescent hospital, and she told me that I looked like my mother even though she only saw my mother once about 40 years ago—what a remarkable memory at 90 years old.

Imam Haroon and Sister Luella had one daughter, Dorothy. She married and had three sons, who grew up to be knowledgeable and handsome young men. The oldest and my daughter were about the same age, and he was my student at the

Sister Clara Muhammad School. Dorothy was a cosmetologist, who worked from home, and I was one of her customers.

After her sons became adults, she helped care for her mother's sister; then she took art classes, which she had wanted to do for many years.

Dorothy's youngest son, Ojiki, married and made her the proud grandmother of three grandchildren.

I knew that Dorothy was not feeling well; however, I did not know the seriousness of her condition. So, when I learned she passed away, I was startled.

After his mother's death, Ojiki had more time to concentrate on his grandmother's health issues. When he decided to take his grandmother home, he encountered opposition from the nursing facility personnel and had to retain an attorney. He hired a 24/7 nursing staff who cleaned her thoroughly, and then he was able to kiss her cheeks the way he did when he was a child. Finally, he cared for her in her own home and bed.

When I heard what he did, I called and told him how proud I was of him. In less than a year, his grandmother also passed away. I pray that Allah also grants her Paradise for all her honorable deeds and that Allah rewards Ojiki for his caring and concern.

Brother Randolph and Family

Brother Randolph and Sister Marie's daughter, Gwendolyn, became a petite, attractive young lady. What a brilliant young lady! She attended elementary school at the University of Islam, graduated, attended several junior colleges, then went to Cal State Dominguez Hills, majored in Art and Physiology, and earned two master's degrees. She married and had two children, a boy, and a girl.

She used her skills to make outfits for herself, her mother, and her daughter. She also specialized in making clothing for the children at the masjid and her sisters in Islam. I saw some of the beautiful garments she designed and made.

Gwendolyn was devoted to her parents, and as they aged, she cared for them, especially her mother, who had hip replacement surgery, which resulted in decreased mobility. She had to monitor her father, who loved sweets. The day that I visited them, she baked some cookies.

I was not in frequent contact with the family after 1975; however, I occasionally visited them when I heard that her mother had hip replacement surgery. She took her family to Chicago's 2013 annual Savior's Day event.

Gwendolyn had a long-term illness and passed away in August 2013; several years later her mother passed away, then her father passed away. May Allah bless the family for all their honorable deeds.

Brother Frank and His Family

Brother Frank Lemons was another good friend of Ronald's when he lived in California. Ronald told him a lot about me and Brother Frank was eager to see me. He called me Queen Delores.

He married after we moved to California, and he and his wife had four daughters. They named their first daughter, Saudia, after my daughter. The Lemons' children attended the University of Islam until 1975, then the children stopped coming to school and my daughter did not see them again until 2021.

Brother Frank passed away in 1975. His widow and daughters are doing well, and his widow has some grandchildren.

Brother Arthur (Nuri Salaam) and Others

Brother Arthur, a friend of Ronald's, sustained life-long injuries on April 27, 1962. His wife, Donzella, lived in Tennessee; however, she came to California and stayed with him during his recovery. We blended since both of us were experiencing anxiety and grief. They had three children, two sons, and one daughter.

She became employed at the Department of Public Social Services (DPSS), where I worked. We went to lunch together and had an opportunity to talk and relieve our stress. She already had a degree and continued working on her teaching credential until she completed it; then, she started teaching. We remained good friends.

She and her husband divorced, and Arthur remarried Chandra, who shared his belief. Arthur and Chandra also had two sons and one daughter, who blended into one peaceful family.

I met Chandra in the late 1960s. She has a passion for education and learning. She and Arthur went to Memphis, Tennessee, in 1975 to spearhead a community transition from the Nation of Islam's nationalistic emphasis to the practice of the five principles of Islam proper, under the leadership of Imam W. Deen Mohammed.

Nuri made Hajj (Pilgrimage to Mecca) in 1978. By 1979, with their limited funds, trained Montessori personnel, retired teachers, and blessings from Allah, they opened a Clara Muhammad School with four grade levels. Chandra and Nuri remained in Memphis until 1983.

In 1987, while pursuing a master's degree at Cal State University Dominguez Hills, Chandra did her school counseling internship at Fremont High School in Los Angeles. Additionally, from 1988 to 1989, she worked for Compton Unified School District as a ninth-grade counselor at Dominguez High School.

Nuri's real estate quest and entrepreneurial vision led him to Atlanta in hopes of establishing an African Market Place.

From 1989 to 1996, Chandra worked for CMS/WD Mohammed High as a guidance counselor and teacher. She laid the foundation for 10th-grade students to graduate from HBCUs like Spelman, Morehouse, Tuskegee, Emory, Duke, Harvard, Georgetown, Stanford, Vanderbilt, Morehouse School of Medicine, Emory Law School, GSU, CSU, etc.

These graduates became lawyers, doctors, teachers, engineers, entrepreneurs, imams, judges, architects, and diplomats. She also worked at Morris Brown College's Trio Summer Program and Clark Atlanta's Master Institute, recruiting talented college students to get their doctorate degrees. Chandra graduated from Clark Atlanta University, earning her doctorate in Educational Leadership. In 1990, Chandra traveled throughout Morocco with Norman, aka Yusuf Wazeerud-Din, before performing Hajj.

Nuri passed away in Long Beach, California, in 1997. However, Chandra continued cultivating the youth wherever she resided, hosting Rites of Passage and Princess Ball programs.

Chandra worked for Long Beach Unified School District at Jordan High School from 1998 to 2014 as a school counselor and an African American History & Culture advisor.

She founded the African American History & Culture Foundation (AAHCF) in 2014, to continue escorting youth on affordable tours to eighty colleges, HBCUs, and ten historical sites and museums from 2006 to 2021.

AAHCF honored over 215 Community Heroes, whom she calls Elder Queens & Kings. She has a passion for elders and a desire to preserve their contribution.

Chandra is the lead archivist of the Imam Haroon and Louella Abdullah Archive Library at Masjid Al-Shareef of Long Beach, which houses Dr. Ramona Zakiyyah Muhammad's Scholarly Collection of Muslim American History. The library is due to open in the spring of 2022.

Sister Captain Mamie and Her Family

Sister Captain Mamie remained the MGT captain until the Nation of Islam changed in 1975, and MGT was not necessary in Al Islam.

Sister Mamie and her husband had three sons. One of her sons is married and has several children and grandchildren. He is also the Imam of Masjid Bilal Ibn Rabah.

Sister Mamie passed away, and some years later, her husband also passed away. May Allah accept their honorable deeds.

Sister JoAnn and Family

Sister JoAnn, who gave me maternity clothes when I was pregnant, is married and has a large family, including grand and great-grandchildren. After many years, she recently retired from the post office and became secretary of Masjid Bilal Ibn Rabah. Now she is at home enjoying her retirement.

Sister Anna and Family

I met Sister Anna, her daughter, Sister Helen, and Sister Helen's six daughters, who ranged in age from late teens to adolescence. Later, sister Helen had another daughter.

When Sister Helen's daughters were older, they married and had children. One daughter did not have any children. Marie married Brother Robert, brother of Brother William, paralyzed for life, on April 27, 1962; the police shot Robert multiple times.

Three of Sister Helen's daughters are now grandparents. The oldest daughter, Marie, babysat for me a brief period. Sisters Anna and Helena are deceased; however, I am still in contact with Marie and Janice.

Sister Sherell

Ruth Sherell, Captain Edward's sister, and I stayed in touch for some years, after I met her. I knew and enjoyed knitting and crocheting, and I taught her how to crochet. After she married and had a daughter, I helped Ruth crochet a sweater and booties for her baby. I have not seen her lately, but her niece, Deanne told me several years ago that she was doing well.

Sister Mary and Brother Ike

Sister Mary and her husband, Brother Ike, and Sister Barbara and her husband, Brother Nathaniel, owned a restaurant on 51st and Main, frequented by many Muslims, especially after the Wednesday, Friday, and Sunday meetings.

Mary was a music major who graduated from Grambling State University and then moved to California. Mary met and married Ike Charles Goldsmith, and both became members of the Nation of Islam.

Mary and I became friends, and she was kind and gregarious. She and Ike had a daughter and a son, and her daughter married and had a son.

Mary taught at the Muslim School, and years later, she was a substitute teacher for the same school district where I worked and occasionally substituted for me.

Brother Ike passed away some years ago; Sister Mary passed away in December 2018. May Allah bless both for their honorable deeds.

Brother Nathaniel and Sister Barbara

Brother Nathaniel and Sister Barbara had three children, one daughter and two sons. Their children married and had several children. Unfortunately, Brother Nathaniel passed away several years ago. One of Sister Barbara's sons lived in Texas, and she and her daughter moved to Texas. I have not heard anything concerning her, but I hope she is well. May Allah bless them for their honorable deeds.

Brother Khalil Karim Sr. and His Family

I met Brother Khalil, an entrepreneur, in the 1960s. He and his wife, Diane, had three children, two daughters and one son; all of them are grown and have children. His oldest daughter and my daughter, Saudia, attended the same school and were good friends for many years. Brother Khalil knew my daughter's father, and when he saw me, he asked me about my daughter, Saudia, which impressed me.

After graduating high school, Brother Khalil became a barber by trade. However, his family's increase necessitated additional income, so he began creating a line of hair care products, *Magnificent Product*, which fitted the African American market. His creations included the first natural comb or afro pick and a line of hair care products. He was in business for many years and acquired sufficient funds to care for his family adequately.

Brother Khalil had a long-term illness and passed away. May Allah bless him for helping his employees to care for their families.

Jamil Shabazz

Jamil became a member of the Nation of Islam in 1972. He was a true entrepreneur who owned and operated several businesses and was one of the first African American owners of an answering service. He employed several of the youngsters in the community.

Later, he owned the well-known Crenshaw Cafe, where many celebrities and former dignitaries, including Muhammad Ali, Michael Jackson, Stevie Wonder, and even former President Bill Clinton visited.

In 2004, Jamil honed his culinary skills by enrolling in and graduating from La Cordon Bleu, which he shared with his son, Jamil Jr, who is also a chef.

Jamil and Geraldine, both previously married with adult children and grandchildren, married, and remained married for some time. Jamil became ill and stayed in a convalescent facility until he expired.

Geraldine was a creative, talented young lady who taught preschool at Islah Academy, a Muslim School in Los Angeles. She made a small quilt for the main hallway that attracted everyone's attention. Geraldine's classroom was always colorfully decorated.

Geraldine remained in California, taught for eight months, then visited her son and his family in Atlanta, Georgia, where she realized that living costs were less in Georgia than in California; thereafter, she remained in Georgia.

May Allah bless Jamil for assisting people with employment, and may He bless Geraldine for her patience in teaching preschool students.

Naim Shah Sr.

Brother Naim became a member of the Nation of Islam in 1964, at 18 years old, and he was ready and willing to work. He was a squad leader, then a lieutenant at Mosque 27 in Los Angeles, California, and finally, the West Coast Regional Captain responsible for seventeen states. Quite an achievement.

Brother Naim is the oldest of three sons, his father, and a younger brother are deceased, and his 93-year-old mother is still living. Brother Naim's brother and sister-in-law live with Naim's Mother and are her caregivers. What a blessing.

Brother Naim, and his first wife, Jowharah, had four children, three sons, and one daughter; each one he says is unique. In his "*Security Handbook,*" he says that he is grateful to Allah (SWT) for his children's mother blessing him with the children. Jowharah is a health care provider, and she continues to thrive.

His oldest son, Naim Jr., is a Certified Public Accountant. He and his wife, have four children, and have lived in Saudi Arabia for more than ten years, where the children receive an excellent education, and his son is becoming a hafidh. Al hamdulillah.

His second son, Sharrieff, is a graduated attorney from the University of Utah; but now he is a coach at the University of Utah. He is also married and has two sons.

Mesha, his daughter, is married and has two adult children who made her a grandmother. Currently, she is a hairstylist, working towards a nutrition degree at the University of California at Los Angeles (UCLA).

His youngest son and personal physician, Abdul, is married and has three children. Their father, Brother Naim, said Abdul and Mesha plan to merge their two professions when she completes the medical part of her schooling.

May Allah bless all of them with success in their positive endeavors.

Altrecia and Herman

Altrecia and her husband Herman were Ronald's friends whom I met when we moved to California. She had several sisters and one brother. Later, I met two more of her sisters, Inez, Rita, and a nephew, Glen, and his family.

Altrecia and Herman had three children, two daughters, and one son. They moved to Philadelphia in the seventies, where she still lives, and I see her occasionally when she comes to California. Altrecia and Herman also have five grandchildren and several great-grandchildren. Herman is deceased.

Inez has been married; however, she has no children, so she enjoys spending time with her grand and great-grand nieces and nephews. She was the secretary of the University of Islam in Los

Angeles in the 1960s before she worked for IBM and transferred to Philadelphia. IBM moved her back to California in the 1970s.

Now, Inez lives in Atlanta, GA., where her great-nephew Karem, Glen's son, and his family live. She sold her house in Atlanta and purchased a unit in a new senior complex and plans to remain there.

Rita, the youngest child, married and had one daughter. Later her daughter married and had two daughters. She has lived in Seattle, Washington, since the early 2000s. The one thing we all have in common is shopping; we shop until we drop, especially at significant store sales.

Their nephew Glenn still lives in Los Angeles. He is married and has two children; his son lives in Atlanta, close to his aunt, Inez.

Inez's friend, Lancy, was married to Inez's nephew Glenn, and they had a son. Lancy is a bright young lady, and she and Inez are good friends.

Daisy, who lived in Los Angeles, is also a good friend of Inez and mine. She lives between Georgia and Florida; we occasionally see and hear from her.

Sister Geneva

Sister Geneva lived close to the Muslim' school and temple and was also a convenient babysitter for the parents whose young children attended the school. Sister Geneva was a kind, pleasant person who loved children. Sister Geneva's sister, her sister's husband, and three minor sons, also lived in Los Angeles. Sister Geneva had one adult son.

Geneva and my sister Geneva met in Los Angeles when my biological sister came to visit me, and the two of them remained friends. Sometime later, Geneva's sister, Roberta, and her family moved to Chicago. Shortly after that, Sister Geneva moved to Chicago where she and my sister, Geneva, reconnected.

Sister Geneva remarried, her husband passed away, and she lived in Chicago until she passed away. May Allah bless her for all her honorable deeds and grant her a high place in Paradise.

Sister Marva

Sister Marva and her family became members of the Nation of Islam after the brutal attack on April 27th at the temple at 56th and Broadway. She was outraged at the inhumane treatment of the brothers and the killing of Ronald Stokes.

She became a teacher at the University of Islam in Los Angeles, moved to Chicago, continued teaching, and remarried.

We were remarkably close when she lived in Los Angeles and remained when she moved to Chicago. She was an excellent cook, and when I visited the masjid in Chicago, she took me home for dinner. How gracious.

Sister Marva retired from teaching, and a sister told me that she lives with one of her daughters. May Allah bless her for the many years she devoted to educating our children.

Sister Clarice and Family

Sister Clarice was a warm, kind person who illuminated the room when she entered. She always hugged me; she was married and had several children, all of whom held on to the banner of Al Islam.

Before his death, her husband had a period of illness, and Sister Clarice and her children gave him the best care. When sister Clarice's health started declining, her daughters took excellent care of her.

May Allah bless Sister Clarice and her husband and family for supporting the Muslim Community.

Sister Juanita and Family

Sister Juanita was married and had one daughter and three sons. Later, she remarried and had another son. When the Muslim school opened, she enrolled her children and taught at the school.

Her daughter, Darcus was a rapid learner, very intellectual. When she graduated from high school, she attended college. She married early and had three children, two daughters and one son.

She pursued a career in education and became a community college professor. Her oldest daughter followed her. Her son is an artist who paints murals and has murals in Los Angeles. Her youngest daughter is an entertainer.

Sister Juanita and I did not see each other frequently; however, I saw her in 2015 at a gathering at Sister Marshal's house. It was a pleasure seeing her as well as the other sisters. I am glad I saw her because several years later, she expired.

I pray that Allah blesses her for all her honorable deeds.

Sister Janis, Brother Raymond Muhammad, and Family

Like many members of the Nation of Islam I met in California, Sister Janis and I frequently saw each other before we started talking. Sister Janice was a friendly person with a beautiful smile who loved children and let them stay at her house if they behaved.

Sister Janis graduated from Jefferson High School in Los Angeles, the Class of 1957. Shortly after graduating, she married one of her classmates, Raymond Mohammed, and they became members of the Nation of Islam. They had six children: three sons and three daughters.

Sister Janis had occasional gatherings for the post-teens, whom she called young adults, and everyone enjoyed them.

She was a kindergarten teacher at the University of Islam in Los Angeles, Dean of Girls, and in charge of Youth Services. She was at the school for many years.

Then she moved to Pasadena and started attending college. She stayed there for a while then moved to Riverside, CA. She continued her education and was also in charge of youth services, while working as a student counselor. She earned her degree in Human Services and managed the Leading-Edge Learning Center until she became ill. She had a passion for G-d, family, singing, and an exuberant personality.

Her husband, Brother Raymond was admired and respected by the young Muslim men, as demonstrated by their numbers at his funeral. I even saw a brother who previously lived in Los Angeles return for Brother Raymond's service.

Brother Raymond passed away in April 2014; Sister Janis passed away on November 23, 2014. They leave behind numerous grands and great grands. May Allah accept their honorable deeds and grant them Paradise.

Sister Maryam

Sister Maryam, a businessperson, and her two children moved to Los Angeles, California, from Birmingham, Alabama in 1957 to start a new life. She attended Los Angeles Trade Technical College to improve her printing skills. She worked for Los Angeles County USC Medical Hospital for a while. Later, she opened Mar Liz, a successful printing business. She converted a sunporch at her house into a cozy indoor tea and snack room. She opened a cosmetic shop in 2015. She was a marathon runner with the Renaissance Runners and won a bronze medal in 1991.

I called Sister Maryam when I needed repairs done to my rental properties because she had property and knew people who made repairs. She had a cousin who was a retired contractor who repaired and remodeled several houses for me. Sister Maryam and I even considered purchasing some properties together, but we did not.

Sister Maryam and I attended CAIR's annual banquets in Anaheim and other events given by immigrant Muslims. We frequently attended the Annual Testimonial to Leadership Fundraiser Banquet in Los Angeles. She reminded me in advance of the event and secured a driver for us if we traveled long distances or in the evening. I always purchased my ticket from her.

Sister Maryam passed away unexpectedly on September 23, 2017. I miss her and pray that Allah accepts all her honorable deeds and support of Al Islam and grants her Paradise. Amen.

Sister Kay and Her Husband

Husband, wife, daughter, and son. Sister Kay greeted you with a warm smile and gave you a big hug. She has several grandchildren and great-grandchildren.

I saw her at the annual Mothers' Day Celebration in Long Beach and other events at the masjid.

Once, Sister Kay's family gave her a surprise birthday party. Initially, she was annoyed because they did not tell her exactly where they were going, and they knew she did not like secrets. However, when they arrived, she was happy. We had an enjoyable evening with an abundance of food and drinks.

Several times, Sister Kay had a few sisters over for brunch. Her daughter, Sabreen, prepared the food and enclosed a menu with the invitation, enabling the invitees to select their entrée before arriving. How considerate. Additionally, everyone left with a goody bag full of essentials.

May Allah bless her, keep her healthy, and ease her pains.

Sister Betty and Her Family

Sister Betty was one of my babysitters and friends. She was married and had one son and four daughters. However, her son passed away when he was a young adult. One of her daughters and Saudia were close in age and friends. She also has some grandchildren.

I saw Sister Betty at a senior center, and she told me that she was displeased because her children had convinced her to stop driving. She has made the transition, and I pray that Allah will grant her Paradise. Ameen.

Sister Marshal and Her Family

I have known Sister Marshal for many years. She was married and had one son and two daughters. Her husband passed away. After his death, she remarried and had a daughter and a son. She was a preschool and kindergarten teacher, who loved children and lived in a big house often filled with children.

Sister Marshal's children are grown, and she has many grandchildren. Occasionally, I see her oldest daughter and ask about her mother. She says she is feeling well.

Brother Jessie, Sister Barbara, and Family

Sister Barbara and Brother Jesse were two more people who became members of the Nation of Islam after the April 27th melee at the temple.

Barbara was the nurse on duty in charge of the emergency care ward at the Los Angeles General Hospital, where they sent all the brothers who were brutalized at the Temple on 56th and Broadway, in Los Angeles for treatment. She worked on all the brothers, except Brother William, who had no pain due to being paralyzed. In this unprovoked attack, the brothers sustained lifelong injuries.

Sister Barbara cared for the injured brothers; she closed the curtains and blinds to keep the curious out. She heard their overdone comments. She was upset over the comments and glee she heard from Black and white people who worked at the hospital. However, her empathy, sympathy, respect, excellent care, and compassion made a significant difference. All the victims of the "incident" had immediate surgeries except Brother William because he was paralyzed.

Barbara was protective of the brothers during their stay. One of the brothers was shot, Minister Arthur, asked Barbara whether she was Muslim, and she said no. He told her she was, but she was unaware. [2]

They were among the first families to enroll their children in the Muslim school formerly known as the University of Islam, now the Sister Clara Muhammad School (SCMS).

Sister Barbara valued education, as shown by her accomplishments. She received her Bachelor of Science from Cal State University Dominguez Hills and completed a Physician Assistant Program at Charles R. Drew University of Medicine and Science. She was the first president of the Physician Alumni Association at Charles R. Drew University of Medicine and Science.

Sister Barbara's name changed after 1975 to Hafeezah Khadijah Al-Ugdah. When we were younger, among other things, we discussed the need for a senior care facility in our community. However, we could not generate sufficient funds to start the project. She kept me updated on current events in the community.

Brother Jessie, the entrepreneur, had a beautiful smile. He attended and played football at Thomas Jefferson High School in Los Angeles. He was known for his burger stand across from Jefferson High School on 41st Street and Hooper Avenue, also known as *Brother Jesse's Place*. After he outgrew that location, he moved to a new location on 43rd Street and Avalon Blvd. He also was known for his $0.25 burritos and Muhammad Ali Punch at both locations. People enjoyed his previous restaurant next to Temple #27 on Central Avenue for the Fish Karate and Rice Pudding.

Brother Jesse's family gave him a birthday party every December, and I went to most of them. He enjoyed those parties as much as the guests. The food was always excellent and plentiful. The party also allowed me to see his grand and great-grandchildren grow. I miss those parties as I am sure everyone else does.

After retiring from the fast-food business at 63, his love for track and field encouraged him to start walking in marathons. He walked in numerous marathons, including New York, Long Beach, and Los Angeles. He became popular with the public and family as the "Marathon Man." Brother Jesse was named "Superman" by Imam W. D. Muhammad.

Brother Jesse passed away on September 20, 2019, and Sister Barbara followed him on October 16, 2019. Brother Jesse and Sister Barbara were married for 65 years. They had five children, two daughters, and three sons; unfortunately, one son expired. They have several grandchildren and great-grandchildren. Priscilla, their eldest daughter, is the founder and CEO of the University of Islam and Sister Clara Mohammed School National Alumni Association. During the editing of my book, the eldest son expired.

May Allah accept and bless them for all their honorable deeds and grant them Paradise.

Joycelyn Rahman

Joycelyn became a member of the Nation of Islam in San Diego as a teenager with her parents and siblings. Later, the family moved to Los Angeles, where she presently lives. She was one of my students at the Clara Muhammad School in the 1970s.

Joycelyn is an employee at the Bilal Islamic Center, on Martin Luther King and Central Avenue in Los Angeles, where a Charter School is also located.

She is also an entrepreneur and creates gorgeous earrings, necklaces, and bracelets. It is always a pleasure to see her because she greets me with a warm smile when she sees me.

Sister Munirah

Since I have known Sister Munirah, she has been dependable. She is the mother of three adult children and has four-plus grandchildren. Additionally, she is an entrepreneur who had a resale shop with quality merchandise in Leimert Park for many years.

Munirah's daughter is married, and she and her husband have four minor children, both of whom work. Therefore, Munirah takes her daughter's children to school.

She assisted Masjid Ibaadillah in maintaining the building on Jefferson until the masjid relocated to Slauson. Then the Jefferson building became a thrift store that she operated until it closed. In addition, she coordinates the weekly food giveaways and the annual Iftar and Night of Power events.

May Allah continue to bless her for her dedication to the masjid.

Hazel, Joyce (Shaheda), and Families

Hazel and Joyce are sisters raised in Fresno, California. Hazel is the oldest and has one son. Joyce has three sons and one daughter, Quiyamah, who needed a female playmate. When Hazel met my daughter, Saudia, she thought she had found the perfect daughter, an only child; now, she could have her son and a daughter, and Saudia could have brothers. So, Saudia became Hazel's daughter and Quiyamah's playmate.

There was a family in the community whose mother passed away, and no one in the mother's family could keep the boys. So, Hazel and Joyce took care of them until they were grown. They referred to Hazel and Joyce as mother and referred to the children as their brothers and sisters. How generous and caring.

Over the past 55 years, we have disconnected and reconnected from changing phone numbers or addresses, but there was always someone who provided us with current telephone numbers.

Our children have made us grand and great grandparents. Hazel's son has ten children and some grandchildren. With the help of my good sister, Inez, I contacted Hazel in May 2021, after not talking to her for several years. She gave me Joyce's telephone number, but Joyce called me before I called her. Of course, we were delighted to hear from each other and plan to visit soon.

Except for age-related issues, we and our families are doing well and looking forward to seeing each other soon.

Update: I saw Hazel, Joyce, and their family members at a funeral service, May 2022. Despite the occasion, we had a brief, enjoyable gathering.

Sister Aishah and Her Family

Aishah was married and had two teenage children when I met her. She worked for an organization that helped battered and abused females get a fresh start in life.

She was a leader; therefore, she started a non-profit organization; *Advancing Humanity with Assistance and Directions*. She recruited her husband, me, and some other brothers and sisters to assist her with the organization. We generated funds from yard sales and generous donors. An organization let us use one room as a resale store until the building sold.

Aishah was an excellent cook, and when we visited youngsters in juvenile facilities, we cooked food and took it to them. We also went to a male juvenile facility east of Los Angeles during the month of Ramadan and took them food which they enjoyed.

Sister Aishah wanted to make Hajj but needed someone to go with her due to ill health. So, although Sister Asilah and I went to Hajj earlier, she went with Aishah again. Asilah told me that Aishah was sick during Hajj, but she completed the rituals.

When they returned home, the doctor told Aishah she had diabetes. Unfortunately, shortly after returning from Hajj, Sister Aishah was diagnosed with cancer. However, we continued the organization until she passed away.

May Allah bless Aishah for her hard work in Al Islam and for endeavoring to uplift women in need.

Sister Yvonne Ali

Sister Yvonne Ali is a friendly sister whom I have known for many years; however, I knew little about her until I read an article on honorees in the November 18, 2018, "Testimonial to Leadership" fundraiser banquet brochure.

I have known her for a long time, and she always gives me a warm greeting, and we talk. I knew she had a daughter, one

ETCHED INTO MY SOUL

grandson, and one granddaughter, but I did not realize she had these skills:

- Teacher at Wadsworth Elementary School in the 1970s
- Owner of a Boutique Shop
- Part owner of snack shop with her son-in-law in 1974
- Teacher and part-owner of a preschool with her daughter

Ali is in her early-90s and lives with a sister who is her caregiver. I called her and she was asleep. Hopefully, she is well, and inshallah, I will call her again.

May Allah bless her.

Brother Harry and Sister Mable

Sister Mable was one of my reliable babysitters. She and her husband, Brother Harry, had six children: two daughters and four sons. She willingly kept Saudia all night when I had classes that ended after 9pm. Brother Harry was a realtor and remained in that position until he retired.

The children attended the University of Islam, which changed its name in 1975 to Sister Clara Mohammed School. After graduating from high school, they attended schools of higher learning. Some of them married and had children.

Mable became a cosmetologist and was looking for a shop. Fortunately, I was teaching at a skill center, and one of my students had a shop that he wanted to sell. I told Mable about his shop, and she contacted him and purchased it. Of course, I was one of her customers.

One day, about two or three o'clock, she was doing my hair in the shop, and the thought came to me that I should tell her to lock the door. However, before I told her, a man walked into the

106

shop with a gun, and robbed us at gunpoint. That was a very frightening experience. After he left, she locked the door, called her husband, then we left, and she finished my hair at her home. That never occurred again because Mable always kept the door locked. Besides, she moved to another shop.

I see Mable on Friday at Jummah Prayer and Ramadan during Taraweeh Prayer. We talk about our children and grandchildren, and everyone is doing well.

My Babysitters

I must mention two sisters I remember who also helped me when a babysitter gave me short notice of her inability to babysit the next day. Sister Sally and her two daughters, my former students, babysat for me, and I was grateful. Sister Sally is no longer with us, but I pray that Allah accepts all her charitable deeds and grants her Paradise. Her daughters are grown, married, and have their own families. May Allah bless them also.

The other family who assisted me was the Kausar family, Brother Nadine, Sister Alberta, an older daughter, a younger son, and three teens and pre-teen daughters, whom I have known for many years. One of the teenage daughters, Alice, said they enjoyed having a young child in the house.

The parents, the oldest sister, brother, and Alice are no longer with us, but may Allah bless all of them for their help.

Sister Mahasin and Her Family

Sister Mahasin, her husband, and five children lived near Manual Arts High School. She was a cook who enjoyed having people over for dinner. In addition, she is a superb artist.

They had five children: two sons, and three daughters. She moved from her big house, which I liked very much, to a smaller place; however, I still see her at the masjid and other Islamic events.

Once, Sister Mahasin and I attended Night of Power the same night at Masjid Ibaadillah on Jefferson Boulevard, which was informative and productive.

Sister Mahasin, a group of believers, and I journeyed to San Diego to see Imam Muhammad slaughter a lamb. We also traveled to San Diego in April 2008 for a speech given by Imam Muhammad.

Rita and Her Family

Rita is a well-groomed young lady I met in the late 1960s. She was a newlywed. Later, she and her husband had two sons, one of whom is married and has two beautiful daughters.

She started in the business world as an accountant and decided that opening a childcare facility at home would benefit her; therefore, she started her business, enjoyed it, and is successful.

Usually, I see Rita during the month of Ramadan at Taraweeh prayer, and I also see her occasionally on Fridays at Jummah prayer. We recently had a conversation about current events.

Sister Rajeeyah Muhammad

Sister Rajeeyah was a young single parent with three sons and three daughters, whom I met at the temple. She enjoyed cooking and attended Trade Tech for short periods because of frequent illnesses.

Rajeeyah's daughters married and had beautiful children. The oldest daughter has two daughters; the second daughter has two daughters, and the youngest daughter has one son and two daughters. Her youngest son has one child.

I saw most of them at Islamic holidays and the oldest daughter and husband on Fridays at Jummah Service before Covid.

She and Mahasin Shamsiddeen were good friends, and when hospitalized, Mahasin called me, and I visited her.

Allah blessed Rajeeyah to perform the Hajj in 2006. Shortly after her trip, she expired. May Allah accept her honorable deeds, blot out any shortcomings, and reunite her in Paradise with all her family members to dwell there forever. (Ameen!)

Hajjah Arnette (Hajarah) Hasan Hamilton

Sister Arnette grew up in Illinois where she attended elementary and secondary school, then college while working in the evening as an accountant. Her family says she was quiet in public but very vocal at home. Finally, she went to Los Angeles to live with her grandparents.

She married in Los Angeles and had three children: two daughters, and one son. All her children are married and have at least one child. I knew her oldest daughter, Katrina, who is articulate and helped me edit essays.

She continued her education at Los Angeles City College, majoring in business, then changed to cosmetology at Los Angeles Trade-Tech. In addition, she was versatile. She had a daycare, taught social studies at the Sister Clara Muhammad School, and drove a Los Angeles Unified School District bus.

I do not know precisely when I met Sister Arnette and her family nor when they became members of the Nation of Islam or Muslims. However, she was a bright, caring, pleasant individual devoted to Al Islam.

She took sisters to medical appointments or and invited them to her home wherever they needed to have weekly dhikr (remembrance of Allah) meetings.

One Sunday afternoon, on my way to Riverside, a sister called and told me that sister Arnette was in a coma. I stopped by the hospital and prayed for her before leaving for Riverside. Praise be to Allah she survived. Unfortunately, however, she was in a long-term facility for a while.

When she was released, she wanted to spend time with her mother, who lived in Illinois. Therefore, she rented housing, and her mother moved to Los Angeles to live with her.

Her mother, Mrs. Catherine Collins, was a knowledgeable ninety-plus-year-old woman, and we bonded quickly. Next, I took her to a senior center near my house, which had a six-week seminar on coping with chronic ailments. Both of us enjoyed and benefited from the workshop. Occasionally, we had lunch at the center.

Sister Arnette's health declined and she returned to a long-term facility. I visited Mrs. Collins frequently. Unfortunately, Sister Arnette expired, and her mother moved to Detroit to live with her younger sister. I miss them.

I went to Toledo, Ohio, in July of 2019, and I intended to see Mrs. Collins in Detroit, but she became ill and passed away about a week before I arrived. I was sad and disappointed.

I pray that Allah accepts Mrs. Collins and her daughter's virtuous deeds, blots out their shortcomings, and admits them to Paradise.

Work and Education

I needed to start concentrating on advancing in my job and entering college. So, I began working for the County of Los Angeles as a clerk-typist, moved to a transcriber-typist, and then a unit clerk working with one supervisor. I frequently looked on the bulletin board for promotions and took the test for most of them for which I qualified.

I also considered working in the evenings and going to school full-time to expedite my advancement; therefore, I looked for 24-hour county facilities. However, I decided not to work evenings because I would be away from my baby too long.

I worked at different county facilities. I liked Collections the least because it involved harassing people about their debts and they might not have money to repay. Therefore, I did not work there for long.

In August 1965, while working at the Department of Collections, the Watts Riot occurred. It was hot that day, but I could not understand why it was hotter than usual; however, when I got in my car to go home and turned on my radio, people were rioting in Watts, California. In the background, all I could hear was, 'burn, baby burn.' I hurried, picked up my baby, and went home. The riot lasted from August 11th through 16th.

The curfew was supposed to be in Watts, but I lived in Leimert Park, and our area was also part of the curfew. Fourteen thousand California Army National Guard came; thirty-four people passed away. Additionally, the riot resulted in $14,000 in property damage.

The second riot in Los Angeles occurred after the unmerciful beating of Rodney King on March 3, 1991, by police officers for a traffic violation. The trial was on April 29, 1992, and the officers were acquitted. Hours later, the verdicts were released, and the violence began.

Black people in general, and residents of South-Central Los Angeles in particular, were tired of the brutality and injustice they had endured for many years, so they had to vent. They blocked the South-Central Los Angeles freeways, beat motorists, wrecked, and looted downtown stores and buildings, and set more than one hundred fires. The city was hot.

Rodney King received a substantial settlement; however, I am sure the pain and suffering he endured for the rest of his life did not compensate for his ailments.

Chapter 11
A Change

Two years after Ronald's death, I became lonely and wanted to remarry and have more children. Several eligible brothers were available; however, my child's safety and consideration came first.

I was a single parent with a two-year-old daughter, working full-time and attending college part-time, looking for a trustworthy and capable husband to help me financially, not anyone I had to support. One brother was never married, appealing, but self-centered. This brother married another sister, and they had several children and moved from Los Angeles.

The other brother was a well-known, respected member of the community. He worked, was married before, and had children. From all appearances, he was a responsible, reliable person. We talked for several months, and we had something in common. He got an apartment, then we got married. Although I still had my house on Edgehill Drive, I leased the house.

We had a cordial relationship; therefore, after the lease on the house expired, we moved into the house, and things changed. I still do not know whether moving into my home made a difference or something else; I never learned. We stayed together for less than a year, then divorced.

I believe the choice of marrying him was better than marrying the other brother because after getting married and having two children, he and his wife divorced, and he married a niece of the Honorable Elijah Muhammad in Chicago. One summer, I visited my sister in Chicago and saw him working as a security guard at a bank near my sister's house. After that, I saw him in a Chicago suburban area department store with his second wife. That was the last time I saw him.

In 2022, I saw Brother Garth at a Janaza and needed to get some information to include in my book. During the conversation, he told me where he and his late mother became members of the Nation of Islam. Coincidently, he was from the same area as the brother I mentioned in the previous paragraph. The brother is still an Imam, married and living in Ohio. Small world.

Sold My House

Since I was no longer married, and my sister Geneva had returned to Chicago, I had to find a roommate, which was difficult because people were not compatible or moved in and out, which was bothersome. Finally, Sister Laura, who had a young granddaughter, moved with me; she was immaculate and lived rent-free in exchange for babysitting.

After she left, I sold the house and purchased a smaller home.

Continued with Work and School

I worked five days per week, went to school at least two evenings per week, cared for my child, and went to the temple weekly; therefore, I did not have time for self-pity. I forged ahead with the help of Allah (G-d) and reliable, dependable babysitters.

I continued taking classes in junior colleges until I had the required number of units to transfer to a four-year college. I finished and was pleased with my accomplishment. Then, I started my last two years in college.

I wanted to become a Certified Public Accountant, but statistics were challenging. I did not consider hiring a tutor before changing my major to business education with an accounting option, but that choice worked well.

The county also had a smaller hospital in Los Angeles, John Wesley County Hospital, near Adams and Grand. I worked in the Labor and Delivery Department for several years and enjoyed working there. Occasionally my supervisor allowed me to watch deliveries, which was interesting. Mothers who did not keep their babies did not see them; mothers who kept their babies interacted with them, including breast, or bottle-feeding them.

The county created a new position, Eligibility Worker, and assigned some of the caseworkers' duties to the Eligibility Workers. I frequently monitored the bulletin board and when saw that position and learned that I met the requirements; I applied for, passed the test, and got the position.

I worked from Hollywood to East Los Angeles with seniors we saw annually. If a client could not come to the office for the annual visit, we made home calls and we performed other clerical duties. I documented anything unusual about the client and gave it to my supervisor, and the caseworker followed up.

I visited one Caucasian client in Hollywood who was bedridden, when she heard me talking to her daughter, she asked her, "Is that a nigger?" Her daughter changed the subject. When I returned to the office, I gave my supervisor a write-up regarding the incident and told her she needed to find another worker because I was not returning to visit that client.

I felt uncomfortable walking in large buildings with long hallways where someone could come out of a unit and harm me.

I attended Cal State LA University, so, I scheduled my East Los Angeles home visit for the same days as my classes at Cal State, which worked well for me.

One of my clients from Ann Arbor, Michigan, had a rare abnormality which physicians in Ann Arbor were interested in. The physicians in Ann Arbor contacted The Department of Public Social Services annually requesting notification of our client's condition, because they wanted him, or his remains, returned to Ann Arbor. Because I retired from the County of Los Angeles and became an employee of the Los Angeles Unified School District (LAUSD); I do not know the results.

The 1970s

Ronnie's good friend, Brother William, paralyzed in 1962, started driving again and remarried a sister, Sharon, whom I admired because it takes a solid person to care for someone disabled. Occasionally, after Sunday's meeting, I rode with him to pick up his wife from work.

One day, he called and told me he met a brother who recently completed chiropractor school and might make some money in the future and wanted me to meet him. Brother William and his wife invited the brother, Riza, (aka) Charles, my daughter, and me for dinner. He slightly resembled Ronald, but neither of us mentioned it. Later, Charles told me that when he saw Ronald's picture in the paper in April of 1962, he noticed their resemblance.

We had an introductory conversation. Charles was divorced and had one biological son and two stepdaughters. We exchanged telephone numbers and might have seen each other at the temple.

After I sold my house, the neighborhood where I moved was not as safe as my previous neighborhood, and someone burglarized my home. I called Charles and told him what had happened, so he said, let us get married. He located a brother and his wife; we went to a Justice of the Peace and got married, a prudent decision.

My daughter, Saudia, was eight years old, and I wanted her to be comfortable with Riza (aka Charles); therefore, I let her choose how she wanted to address him. She started calling him Daddy and continued until he passed away. Now she had a daddy like her friends.

Riza was a chiropractor and shared an office in Watts, California with an elderly female chiropractor who was retiring. He remained in his position for many years. He had many Muslim patients who benefited from his treatments. He loved music and had an insatiable appetite for learning; he studied something or played the piano nightly for fifteen minutes.

He promoted a musical group called Commander Funk, whose performers were sparkling and intriguing for children, especially males. The group performed several times at the Roosevelt Hotel in Hollywood. However, it was not successful.

Riza and one of his friends, Moedeen, attempted importing and exporting heavy-duty equipment overseas. However, after leasing an office in Beverly Hills and securing their first order, the import and export law changed, which ended their business.

Since Riza spoke Arabic, he knew some foreign Muslims. We visited and attended some of their culturally enriching functions. Of course, he could communicate with the brothers because he knew the language, and the sisters and I verbalized the best we could.

To Riza, learning was a life-long process; additionally, he wanted to hone his knowledge of Arabic; therefore, he hired a gentleman from Egypt to come to the house five days a week before he went to work to teach him Arabic. Consequently, his knowledge and understanding of Arabic improved immensely.

Riza was also conscious of his health. He went to a men's spa once a week and to the gym twice a week and watched his eating habits. He also reminded me of my diet, even though I was never overweight. He frequently ate at a restaurant owned by a brother, Jamil, with whom he became familiar. The restaurant served various food daily. Occasionally, I ate there.

Riza became the minister at the temple in Pasadena, California, an ideal position since he enjoyed teaching. English was his primary language; however, he was fluent in Spanish, French, and Arabic. The believers wanted him.

The temple in Pasadena was a close-knitted group. Several couples were among the group, and a few were single brothers and sisters. I remember one of them, Brother Aaron and Sister Delores, newlyweds. I still see them occasionally.

Later, they had two sons and one daughter. Now, they are grandparents. Aaron owns a real estate broker business in Altadena, California. His oldest son is a CPA, and his youngest son is a real estate loan processor and recently became a contractor.

Other members were Brother Bruce, his wife, Shaheda, and their six minor sons, Sister Salima and her family, Sister Sum'aku H, Sister Darina and her family, and Sister Jameelah Abdullah Yusuf.

When I moved to California, Sister Maryam, a delightful person, and her family lived in the Pasadena Altadena area. She has a son, Che'; later, she remarried and had four daughters.

Che' owns a hardwood floor business and does excellent work. He installed floors in several units for me. I have not seen Sister Maryam since the beginning of the Pandemic; however, I saw Che' last year. Inshallah, I will see her soon.

Changes in the Nation of Islam

The Nation of Islam's leader, the Honorable Elijah Muhammad, passed away in February 1975, and his son, Wallace Deen Muhammad, replaced him. His death was shocking to many of us.

First and most importantly, we had to learn Islam. Imam Warith Deen Muhammad was more than qualified to teach us since he was fluent in Arabic and thoroughly understood Islam and the Holy Quran. We learned the Five Pillars of Islam:

- There is one G-d, Allah; He has no partners or associates.
- How to correctly pray five times per day.
- Pay Zakat - charity.
- Fast during the month of Ramadan, in the Nation of Islam Ramadan was observed in the month of December.
- Make Hajj (pilgrimage) to Makkah once in a lifetime if one can afford to.

Imam Muhammad encouraged us to say our prayers in Arabic; therefore, many followers began learning Arabic.

Believers whose primary language was Arabic started teaching the language to us. Those were exciting times. Along with change comes disagreement, and we also had our share of that, but we strived and progressed.

Imam Muhammad told the believers that we could have Islamic names. So, many former members of the Nation of Islam legally changed their names. Since I had an Islamic last name from birth, I added Daaimah to my first name.

Chapter 12
Working in Education

I retired from the County of Los Angeles and started working for LAUSD (Los Angeles Unified School District). I was near completing my bachelor's degree and wanted to become a teacher; therefore, I thought the change might be helpful. I finished the two prerequisite classes I needed to become a teacher: one semester classroom observation with a credentialed teacher and one semester as a teacher with another credentialed teacher.

Additionally, I began working on my master's degree. My advisor told me I could get a reading specialist credential with my master's degree by taking several more classes and I did. One of the requirements was teaching reading to a juvenile in a juvenile facility which did not appeal to me, but I fulfilled the requirements. However, I was not comfortable walking across the juvenile campus alone, which I had to do after several visits. After completing all the requirements, I received my master's degree and a reading specialist credential.

Next, I decided to teach at my daughter's private religious school, where only a degree was needed. I wanted to give back to my community before teaching in public school.

The school was the University of Islam, renamed the Sister Clara Muhammad School in 1975. The first principal was Brother Robert. His wife was Sister Alice, and they had three or four sons and one daughter.

When I worked there, Sister Halima was the principal. She was very dedicated and caring, encouraging all students to achieve their maximum potential. She was also concerned about and assisted her staff members in any way she could. In addition, she loved to cook, especially Asian food.

She had a two-and-a-half or three-year-old daughter, Qiyamaa, and two sons. Her daughter, Qiyamaa, came to school daily and stayed in the Preschool room until she was ready for kindergarten. After that, she attended Sister Clara Muhammad until she graduated from high school. Qiyamaa received her bachelor's and Master of Science Degrees from California State University at Dominguez Hills, majoring in health care.

She has worked in the healthcare field at Kaiser Permanente for twenty-two years. She has abundant operational and leadership experience and was promoted on September 20, 2021, to Director of Laboratory/Pathology Operations for Irvine Medical center. After graduating from college, she married and had three children, two daughters, and one son. Her parents have retired and are enjoying their grandchildren. Congratulations Qiyamaa!

Sister Halima has passed on.

Sr. Artice, The School's Secretary

The School's Secretary was Sister Artice, who had three daughters and two sons. One of her daughters, Nona and my daughter, Saudia, were friends.

Sister Artice was compassionate about education, including higher education, and she was instrumental in promoting college education for her own children as well as other youth. Her children each had at least a bachelor's degree, and her oldest daughter, Tanya, was brilliant. After graduating from UCLA, she continued her education in Washington, DC, and became a physician.

Sister Artice assisted many students in acquiring higher education. She was also concerned about individuals. One evening, during the month of Ramadan, close to sunset, I stopped at her house to leave a package. She asked me whether I had broken fast. I told her I was going to the masjid near her house to break my fast. She told me to go to the bathroom and wash my hands. When I came out of the bathroom, she gave me a snack. How caring.

Although she is no longer with us, we still appreciate all her excellent deeds and pray that Allah accepts them and grants her Paradise.

Other Faculty at the School

Twelve plus teachers worked at the school, but I only remember a few of them. I remember Brother Donald, an English teacher, because we simultaneously taught at two different schools. He was married and had several children. His wife, Sharon, was also a teacher.

Brother Donald is a poet and an author who has published more than twelve books, including one book, *Crips*, which depicts the gangs in South Central Los Angeles. He was familiar with the gangs in South Central, and he also understood their language. The gang members respected him, and some converted to Al Islam. Also, some of his former students came to his 75th birthday party in Los Angeles from out of state.

Occasionally, we encountered each other at Cal State Los Angeles while taking graduate classes. We stopped, chatted for a few minutes then we were on our way.

Brother Donald transferred from the University of Islam to Manual Arts High School in 1972. I started teaching at Manual Arts High School in 1979. I saw him and his family frequently at the Masjid. When I taught at Manual Arts High School, two of his daughters were my students for a brief time.

When I met Brother Donald in 1972, he and his wife had two or three children. Now, they have seven grown children and six grandchildren. He assisted me once with my manuscript when I needed help; however, I have not seen many people since Covid 19 began.

Sister Ameerah

Sister Ameerah Abdul-Mujeeb, aka Andrea Victoria Johnson, was another intellectual educator who became a member of Al Islam and a teacher at the Sister Clara Muhammad School.

She went to elementary, junior high, and high school in Los Angeles. Next, she attended California State University and earned a Lifetime Standard Teaching Credential; and became an elementary school teacher.

Early in her career, she received specialized training in Phonics when she realized that many minority students had difficulty reading. She taught at the University of Islam briefly, then took a vacation. She returned as an English teacher and became the assistant principal in 1976. After several years, she became principal and held that position for four years.

She traveled all over the nation studying the teachings of Imam Warith Deen Muhammad while representing the Islamic Education Institute of Los Angeles.

Ameerah was married and had two daughters, one son, and ten grandchildren. One daughter has four children, and one has six children, and I do not know whether her son has any children. Both of her daughters are educators.

After leaving Sister Clara Muhammad School, she worked for 17 years for the Los Angeles Unified School District; then she retired.

Ameerah passed away on March 27, 2005. I pray that Allah blesses her for the many years and hard work she spent educating young people.

Sister Karen English

Sister Karen English is an elementary school teacher who taught at the Muslim schools in Chicago and Los Angeles, California, and has written children's books for many years. She is the mother of four children and has four grandsons.

She is retired and spending time with her 101-year-old mother, who still reads novels. May Allah bless her for the many children she helped to educate.

Other Teachers at the Clara Muhammad School/aka The University of Islam

Fahida

We became acquainted after completing our bachelor's degrees in the early 1970s. In 1971 and 1972, she taught third grade at the University of Islam on Central Avenue in Los Angeles, and she taught at the University of Islam in Compton from 1975 to 1976.

My teaching at the University of Islam was a unique experience because I knew many parents personally, making it easy to communicate with their children; this relationship also helped their educational experience.

Many of the students who attended the school were bright. One student graduated at 14 years old and attended USC. These students applied themselves, were serious about education, graduated, attended schools of higher learning, became physicians, and majored in computer science. I taught at that school for approximately five years.

Zaheerah

Sister Zaheerah, her husband, and six children came to California in the late 1950s and became members of the Nation of Islam in the Los Angeles area. She was among the first to enroll all her children in the Nation of Islam school, the University of Islam (U of I). All her children attended the U of I or the SCMS; four graduated from one of those schools, and five have advanced degrees. She believed education is one of the best ingredients for a successful life and encouraged everyone to achieve their maximum potential.

Her son Bennie, now Omar, graduated from SCMS in the 1970s, became a physician's assistant, and retired in the 2000s. Congratulations to you.

Her oldest daughter, Nayawiyyah, one of my former students is a professor at a University in Long Beach, California.

She has almost completed her Ph.D. in Education. So, congratulations to you, also.

Sister Zaheerah's youngest daughter, Aqueelah, teaches in the Long Beach school district in Long Beach, California, where one of my cousins taught. I am sure her other children are also doing well.

She allowed many students who lived far from the school to stay with her family. This enabled them to benefit from a Muslim environment and a religious education. Besides, she took in and cared for many children over the years.

Sister Zaheerah's biological sister son, Hasan, was also my student. Hasan is in the computer technology field, married, and has children. Whenever he sees me, he greets me and says, "There is my teacher." Thank you, Hasan.

In addition, they had other children who attended the school but were not in my class.

Sister Zaheerah was well-known for raising funds for SCMS in Compton with her bake sales, candy drives, barbecue dinners, and desserts. She was an excellent cook, and I enjoyed eating her food.

She held various positions at the SCMS and assisted in selecting the staff members. Finally, she established the school in Compton; and helped with Masjid Al Shareef's Sunday school.

Sister Zaheerah is no longer with us, but we will never forget her charitable deeds and kindness. May Allah bless them and grant her a high place in Paradise.

Chapter 13
New Careers

In 1976, The National Association for the Advancement of Colored People (NAACP) opened a training center in Southwest Los Angeles. The supervisor of the New Careers Center, Mr. Nash, needed an instructor with clerical experience. I worked in various clerical positions and had my bachelor's degree in business education. After reviewing my resume, he called and told me that I was just the person he needed and hired me. Finally, I was able to apply my training and do what I enjoyed.

The instructors taught touch typing, spelling, proofreading, and how to write resumes. One instructor schooled the students on job interview techniques, proper dress, grooming, and mannerisms for interviews. She also had mock interviews.

NAACP New Careers was a government-funded project, and our success depended on the number of students who secured employment after training. We had a high success rate because we recruited people we knew, and with whom we became acquainted. I am still in contact with several people I knew who got jobs; that was gratifying.

Moving Along

I began teaching middle school for the Los Angeles Unified School District in 1979. Most of LAUSD's beginning teachers substitute before they got a permanent position.

Substituting worked like this: the assignment desk called around 6:30am to give you the assignment. When you checked out at the end of the school day, the clerk told you whether you were needed the next day. If the students were unruly, I declined the offer.

I was a substitute teacher for one semester and had the district not given me a permanent position, I do not believe I would have returned because substituting was difficult. However, I was assigned a full-time job for the 1979 fall semester and remained until I retired in 1999.

My first full-time assignment was at Lincoln High School in Lincoln Heights, a Hispanic area with a small percentage of Asians and Vietnamese who recently came to the United States. Business education was my major, and I was most qualified to teach the subjects in that department. The students were cooperative and eager to learn; however, the Vietnamese students' limited knowledge of English impeded them. So, I partnered them with one of their peers who English language skills were better, which helped.

Lincoln was in an area with lots of gangs. Occasionally, one or more students' lives would sadly end during the weekend, and Mondays started dismally.

After teaching for five years at one school, an employee could transfer to another school if there was a vacancy. I learned much and enjoyed the experience at Lincoln High School; however, I wanted to share my expertise with the students in South Central

Los Angeles, many of whom resembled me. Therefore, I transferred to Manual Arts High School after teaching at Lincoln for five years. I remained there until I retired.

Manual Arts High School was less than five miles, via surface street drive, from where I lived. Whereas Lincoln High School was fifteen miles from my home, mostly freeway. Schools have parents/teachers' meetings twice a year, and when I taught at Lincoln, I was there from 7:50 am to 8:00 pm, which is a long day. When I taught at Manual Arts, I went home before the Parent Teacher meeting, and returned to school for the meeting.

In 1984, seventy-five percent of Manual Arts students were Afro-Americans, twenty-five percent were Hispanics, and a five percent or less were Asians. When I retired in 1999, the student population was about seventy-five percent Hispanics and twenty-five percent Afro-Americans.

Some students came to school to learn, and others came because it was a requirement. Students who wanted an education worked diligently to earn good grades and achieve their goals. Working with students who were serious and realized the value of a good education was delightful.

Teaching at Manual Arts allowed me to attend sport games, and I especially enjoyed attending basketball games. During the latter part of the 1980s, Manual Arts won championship games, which was extremely exciting.

Additionally, I participated in other extra-curricular activities, such as the senior prom. I enjoyed seeing the students in a non-school environment and in formal dress. Graduation was another event I attended while teaching at Manual Arts. I also went to Senior Night, especially when I had senior homerooms. It meant a great deal to the students to see their teachers at non-mandatory events.

There were good times and tough times, but the good were more prevalent than the bad.

The 1980s

Numerous things occurred during the decade of 1980.

The number of limited English-speaking students increased rapidly, and the School District wanted teachers to learn basic Spanish. As a result, the district offered beginning Spanish classes after school in various areas. In addition, you could go to Mexico to take Spanish classes; I did both for three years.

The first year, I went to Mexico City, Mexico for three weeks, stayed in a hotel, and dined out, which was okay. During the week, I learned the language and the culture. On the weekends, I toured the city via public buses, which was interesting because the neighborhoods changed from well-built brick homes to cardboard boxes within a few feet of each other in some areas.

The thing I did not like about Mexico was the lack of sanitation. The streets downtown were dirty, and rats ran around during the day, terrifying me. However, I returned to Mexico the following year.

The second trip was better. I registered through the University of San Diego Extension School which included housing. I stayed with a single mom who had two unruly minor sons, and she left them with me the first Saturday night I was there. Since I did not come to Mexico to babysit, I called the office on Monday, told them what occurred, and requested other housing. They complied.

The new location was not much better. It was a large house divided into two sections. One side was for the females, and one was for the males. I was in the front area on the female side. Therefore, the women had to pass my bed to get to theirs. Since I retired early, when they came home, they disrupted my sleep. Consequently, I moved again.

The last family I stayed with had a large house with a two-bed single unit downstairs occupied by a young lady who was seldom there, which was perfect.

The families provided breakfast and dinner for the students, and we bought our lunch. Across the street from the dwelling was a grocery store with a deli; therefore, I went there if I desired something different for dinner.

On my third trip to Mexico, I attended classes at the University of San Diego Extension School which oversaw the registration and housing arrangements. Native language speakers taught the classes, from 9:00 am to 12:00 pm, five days per week. As a result, I increased my vocabulary and improved my pronunciation.

The living arrangement for this class was good. I stayed with a family in a middle-class neighborhood near a park. The house was neat, clean, and organized; the host was gracious and prepared well-balanced meals. I shared a two-bed medium-sized bedroom with another female. After class, I went to the park, studied, and enjoyed the sunshine.

A group of students traveled to beautiful Guadalajara one weekend. We had an enjoyable weekend.

The third trip was the most productive and organized for me. During the school year, I continued taking the district's classes, and some of my students assisted me, so I survived.

Real Estate Ventures

I became interested in real estate in the mid-eighties when I heard one of my coworkers telling someone that she and her husband purchased a duplex which helped them pay for their mortgage. What an innovative idea, I thought, and HUD foreclosures were plentiful, but I did not make much progress.

The first house that I purchased was with my late husband, Ronald T. Stokes, in 1962. Unfortunately, he only lived there for 27 days before the police brutally murdered him. I bought a smaller house around 1967. I remarried, and my husband and I bought several other homes.

Then I purchased income properties alone. Finally, in 1970, I bought a small house in South Central Los Angeles and kept it until I married Riza, and we bought another house.

Brother Nazim and his family, who moved from Los Angeles to Arizona, knew a realtor who wanted to buy a restaurant, but he needed funds. One of his clients was retiring from real estate and wanted to sell three properties. Brother Nazim called and asked whether I was interested in purchasing the properties.

I learned that the best way to purchase property is to finance it yourself. Therefore, I borrowed funds from my annuities and put a down payment on two properties. One of the properties had a small balance; hence, I paid the owner the balance and divided the remainder of my funds between the other two properties. They were Section 8 properties, and the city of Phoenix mailed the rent to me unless the tenant paid part of the rent which they sent to me.

The terms of the annuity that I borrowed were for five years, with quarterly payments. After I paid my annuity loans, my debt decreased, then I waited several years, sold my out of state properties and purchased properties in California.

When I owned the properties in Arizona, I hired a realtor who had the payment of one of the properties transferred to her office. Since I was taking more interest in my investments, I had to move the funds back to me. Additionally, she claimed to have installed a new heating system in the house, but the tenant called and told me that the realtor did not install a heating system. Consequently, I had to go to Arizona and sue her, and I won. You must be careful because not everyone is honest.

I picked up a realtor's flier who sold out-of-state property, in a bank where I had an account. She had several properties in my price range in the Carolinas, and I purchased two with low down payments. Then I hired a property manager in the Carolinas area to manage them.

One of the tenants did not pay the rent, and the property manager told me that since I lived a long distance from the property, it would be better for me to sell the property. So, he gave me a discount on his commission, and I sold the property.

The realtor-broker in Greer, South Carolina, rented the house to a lady who stayed there while I owned the unit, but she would not purchase the property even though it would have been less expensive to own than rent. Unfortunately, we could not determine why she did not want to buy it.

I kept the other property in Greer, South Carolina until August 2016, nineteen years longer than I kept any out-of-state rental. The property manager and the realtor were honest and professional. He encouraged me to keep the property until it increased, I did, then he sold it.

When you buy out-of-state real estate, you meet different brokers through various people. For example, Roberta, who moved to California from Seattle, Washington after the death of her husband to assist her recently divorced daughter with twin infant girls, introduced me to a broker in Houston who only sold condominiums. I purchased a condominium and sold it after about ten years. Roberta bought several; unfortunately, she lost money and was unable to retrieve it. Roberta also had two or three adult sons.

By 1997, prices of property in California began to decrease. The realtor from whom I purchased the two properties in the Carolinas sold me a triplex in Leimert Park that I tried, unsuccessfully, to buy from another realtor. I lived in one unit and rented the other two. That same year, I acquired three houses in Moreno Valley and the Inland Empire of California.

I bought one of the houses for my daughter in my name, then transferred it to her. I bought VA properties in Moreno Valley, and the Inland Empire in the mid-1970s, where the properties were inexpensive and plentiful. In those years, once I purchased property from the VA and established a good record, it was easy to get more; however, that no longer exists.

I learned important lessons about selecting tenants from the tenants in the Inland Empire. First, they did not maintain the property. After a tenant lived in one of the houses for a year, I had to totally rehab it.

Lesson Learned: Pay a realtor to do your screening!

In 1999, I purchased another repo triplex in California on 62nd and La Tijera. I drove through that area frequently on my way home from Spanish classes in West Los Angeles and wished I could live there, and I did.

In the early 1990s, I took graduate classes at Cal State LA., and on my way home one evening, I saw a flier advertising a real estate club meeting, which was interesting; therefore, I grabbed one. The sessions met in Culver City Senior Center, close to where I lived. So, I went.

The president of the club, Dr. Marshall Reddick, was a professor at California State University and a real estate broker who believed that everyone should have real estate in their portfolio.

Doctor Reddick's Association had real estate brokers, salespeople, and discount maintenance crews in the cities where his clients' purchased properties.

When he filed his first income tax after purchasing a property, Dr. Reddick said he was pleasantly surprised to see his refund and used the money to purchase another property. After that, he continued purchasing property with his tax refunds until he amassed more than one hundred properties all over the United States by the early 2000s.

In 1994, I purchased my first property in Jacksonville, Florida from the Marshall Reddick Real Estate Association. It had three bedrooms and two bathrooms. I kept the house for almost ten years. When the tenant moved, I sold it. I never saw the house, but the property manager took diligent care of it and sold it for me when it became vacant.

I purchased my last two properties from the Reddick Real Estate Association in 2006, a house in Indianapolis, Indiana, and a condominium in Archdale, NC. Unfortunately, both properties were failures. Hence, I sold the property in Indianapolis before the property manager rented it.

I do not know why the property manager in North Carolina never rented the unit for a year. However, I talked to the realtor and Dr. Reddick regarding the matter but never received a reasonable answer.

One of my realtors in Los Angeles found a realtor in North Carolina who sold the property on my behalf. Of course, I lost money on that transaction, incurred a loss, and wrote off monies lost. That was the end of my business with Dr. Reddick.

I did not know Sister Elaine was interested in the Ladera Heights area until we talked, and she told me she wanted to live in the area for a long time. I had a realtor I knew look for a property in the area. The realtor found a triplex that the owner was eager to sell, and we liked the property and made an offer that the owner accepted. Then Sister Elaine, her son, and I purchased the triplex in Ladera in 2000.

Sister Elaine and her son still live there. I sold my unit in 2008 and purchased another condominium a block from there in 2009. I am presently living in the last property I bought in January 2013. This property was the riskiest property that I have purchased. Usually, I do not respond to solicitors regarding my property; I just put their mail in the trash. But this letter was different from the ones I usually receive. The realtor did not list properties; instead, he asked people whether they were interested in selling their property; if so, he would try to find a buyer. That seemed practical to me. I was interested in finding a larger triplex, so I accepted the offer.

Therefore, the realtor and I immediately started looking for available triples. He listed the property on La Tijera and sold it within a month without a sign in the front yard. Since I had not lived in the property for more than two years, I had to purchase a similar property within 180 days of the sale to decrease my sales taxes.

One evening while browsing on the internet, I found a bank-owned property that I had been interested in for several months listed for sale. The realtor, George Paul, looked for default properties in county records, while I looked on the computer for properties for sale. I immediately called George Paul and gave him the contact information; he called the lender and began the purchasing process.

The property was bank-owned, and the bank's realtor was not helpful. She said the tenants did not want to show the property, which I later learned from one of the tenants was not accurate. Additionally, convention lenders do not fund property without appraising the interior of the property. Hence, if I wanted to purchase the property, I needed a hard money loan, which is risky. George Paul told me his property owner was a hard money lender, but after seeing his offer, I declined.

The monthly interest rates on hard money loans are twelve or more percent monthly; therefore, you must exercise due diligence when selecting hard money lenders because all of them are not candid.

I needed to find an honest realtor I knew or had used previously. The Shakoor's came to my mind. I have known them for many years, and Aaron Shakoor is truthful, and his sons follow him.

I called Jihad Shakoor, Aaron's son, who found me an honest hard money lender who gave me a loan for the length of time I needed, which was one month. The other hard money lender wanted to keep the loan for a year, with that high payment could have resulted in my losing the property. Jihad also sold a condominium for me.

My Trip to Hajj

Hajj, the pilgrimage to the Holy House in Makkah and the fifth basic principle of Islam, should be made once in a lifetime, and Allah (G-d) blessed me to make the pilgrimage to Makkah in 1987.

Asilah, a sister I had known for almost ten years, saw fliers at the Mosque announcing a Hajj seminar, and we took one and attended the workshop, which was informative. We also received instructional material with procedures for performing Hajj.

We needed white garments; therefore, we purchased 100% white cotton cloth, white sandals, and other items for the trip. That was easy but learning when and how to perform the rites was tedious, but we did it with the help of Allah.

Asilah knew a brother from Egypt who made our reservation. We did not understand why he made the reservations three weeks in advance. We flew from Los Angeles International Airport to New York with another group of Muslims from California going to Hajj. After several hours' layover in New York, we boarded an approximate ten-hour flight on Saudi Airlines to Jeddah. If you have ever flown to the Middle East, I am sure you will agree that the Saudi flight is the most tranquil flight you have ever flown. The flight attendants gave us eye masks because they flew east for many hours. The recitation of the Quran was played throughout the plane. Even though I did not know most of the words, the sound was soothing.

We landed in Jeddah, showered, put on our ihram, prayed two rak'as, made our intention for 'Umrah, and started reciting the Talbiyah Dua; (devotional calls after Ihram. Ihram signifies one dressed to enter a state of devotion with the intent of making Hajj or Umrah). Then, we continued our trip to Mecca, where only Muslims are allowed.

My mother sang a song, "I have not been to Mecca," but Fard Muhammad told her that "the streets of Mecca are paved with gold." I looked at the ground, and it was cobblestones; I said, "no, Mama, the streets are paved with cobblestones, not gold."

When we arrived in Mecca, we went to Al-Masjid al-Haram, the largest mosque globally, where we touched and pointed to some artifacts. We walked around the Ka'bah (a cubical box structure) seven times, repeating du'as (prayers requesting things from Allah for yourself and others) and other prayers; called **Tawaf,** circulation of the Ka'bah, and we made two rak'a salat (prayer). If you desire, you can sip Zam Zam water (the water Hager found when she and Ismail were left in the desert by Prophet Abraham. We went to the walkway between the hills of Safa and Marwa, and walked back and forth seven times, called **(Sa'i)**. The above procedures complete the Umrah portion of the Hajj rituals, and you can eliminate some of the Ihram restrictions.

Since we arrived in Saudi Arabia three weeks before Hajj, we had time to go to Medina to visit the Prophet's masjid, where people usually go after Hajj. Unfortunately, people do not see many African American females in that part of the world, and males asked us about our country of origin. When we told them "America," they pointed to their knees, indicating that American females who wore short clothes were amusing.

I had several incidents with males either trying to get in front of me or moving me out of their way. But praise is to Allah (G-d); there was always another brother to put him in his place.

Numerous female Muslims from the Philippines had similar beautiful clothing. They stayed together and would not let anyone break their line. While sitting in the Prophet's masjid, a Philippine sister helped me learn Surahs 113 and 114. I was grateful to her, but my purpose for going to Saudi Arabia was to perform Hajj as perfectly as possible so that Allah, Most High, would accept my performance.

Hajj begins on the eighth day of the month of Dhul Hijjah; we made our intentions to do Hajj, then we bathed and put on our ihram garments again, went to the Ka'bah, performed tawaf, then boarded a bus to Mina. We remained in Mina from Dhuhr (afternoon) prayer to Fajr (the first daily prayer); the following day.

Next, we traveled to the valley of Arafat and remained there in the open terrain praising Allah. After sunset, we traveled to Muzdalifah, combined Maghrib, and Isha'a prayers, and remained there at night. We stood by the sacred monuments at dawn and glorified a sacrifice called Qurbani. We gathered about twenty-one small stones for later use.

We returned to Mina and threw the stones at the pillars called Jamarat Uqbah, which represents Shaytan; then, we should make the Qurbani sacrifice. After that, men should shave their heads, and women can merely cut a lock of hair. Then, we prepared to celebrate 'Eid' and removed the ihram clothes for regular clothes.

The people were so zealous in trying to stone the pillars they missed their target and bumped into others. Many of them were screaming, "Allah-u-Akbar." The crowd was so dense that a sister I met from Washington, D. C., grabbed and held me until we cleared the crowd. One brother in our group from the United States lost his eyeglasses. Praise be to Allah; we made it out safely.

We returned to Mecca on the 10th day, made a tawaf and an optional sa'i, drank Zam Zam water, and returned to Mina for three to four days to stone the various pillars daily. Finally, we did a farewell tawaf in Masjid al-Haram. After the 12th day of Dhul Hijjah, we asked for Allah's forgiveness, and made du'a which completed our Hajj.

A brother notified us that we were departing at twelve that night for Jedda. We quickly completed our final rituals, went to our living quarters, got our luggage, met the brother in the waiting area, rode a bus to Jeddah, and boarded the aircraft to New York.

I did not realize how exhausted I was until I got on the flight and slept until I arrived in Los Angeles. Sister Asilah awakened me, saying the food was good, and asked whether I wanted some. I told her that I only wanted to sleep. When we arrived in Los Angeles, I thanked Allah again for blessing me with a safe return home, my Hajj, and my prayers. AMEN

After I returned home, I stayed in bed and rested for several days.

While I was in Saudi Arabia making Hajj, Saudia got married. Riza convinced her and her friend that marriage is the best life.

The Bittersweet 1990s

Chapter 14
Riza's Devastating Actions

Riza and I had a peaceful ten or more years of marriage. We enjoyed studying and learning. We dined on my birthdays, Mother's Day, and long holiday weekends. We enjoyed Middle Eastern food and frequented halal restaurants in Hollywood. Sometimes after eating, we went to the movies. I took him to dinner on Father's Day or prepared him a delicious homemade meal. He had a favorite candy bar that I kept in the China cabinet. In addition, he brought me gifts when he traveled.

Occasionally, Riza mentioned brothers could have second wives. However, it is difficult to provide for one family; therefore, I do not know how the average male could provide for more than one family; but I *knew* he could not. Consequently, I did not discuss the subject.

Riza made Hajj in 1990. When he returned, he wanted to go to Egypt for a long time and since he had a current passport; he thought this would be a perfect time; hence, he went for several weeks. After returning, he decided to close his chiropractic office, go to Egypt, start an import business, and work in California and Egypt two months each.

I did not feel comfortable with the arrangement, nor did it generate adequate income to pay our bills; nevertheless, he tried it for a few years. Our religion of Islam teaches us not to be suspicious, but something did not seem right to me.

144

Then one day, when Riza was in California, the telephone bill arrived, and I was shocked to see the amount due. When I asked him to whom was, he talking to in Egypt, he replied, "my wife." I was at a loss for words.

I said, "How could you do that to me after all I have endured with you?"

He said, "I did not think you cared."

"Really, and I tolerated your 'I, me' mentality for many years." I exclaimed.

I knew that endless hours of sleepless nights were ahead of me. He told me that no one knew he had another wife, but the truth was, everyone except me knew.

He was the sisters' Imam. When brothers misused their spouses, he told the sisters that the brothers were wrong. I frequently said to him that he had rules for himself and rules for others.

Like many wives, I worked full-time, cooked, cleaned, ironed, and ran errands for him. Where was the appreciation? Where was the gratitude? I stayed in the vacant bedroom until we sold the house.

One day, his wife called, and I answered the telephone. Of course. I asked her whether there was a shortage of males her age in Egypt to marry instead of a man twice her age plus ten years. What did they have in common? I also asked her whether her mother would want her father to marry a female her age. Her response was, "I told him to tell you," then she said, "he loves me," then hung up.

Before I discovered his marriage, Riza had planned for his wife to come to Los Angeles when I was in Chicago in July for the Jordan family reunion. And where did they plan to stay, in the house where I lived? However, Riza's wife became extremely ill and confined to bed for several days; so he cancelled the trip.

Riza and I sold the house, and I moved with my cousin, Louella, because she thought I did not need to be alone. I stayed with her for three months. Then I rented a single unit from one of my coworkers until I purchased a triplex. Even though I was in the apartment alone, I heard the other people; therefore, I did not feel alone.

I did not realize the extent of my pain for countless months. Then, one day, I was sitting on the couch crying uncontrollably; I did not want to feel that way. Hence, I got off the couch and on my prayer rug and told Allah (G-d) that I did not want to feel that way. When I finished praying, I got up, washed my face, and sat back down, and I have never felt that way again.

With the help of Allah, prayer, patience, and perseverance, we can overcome many obstacles. Praise be to Allah.

Life, time, and people go on. Then, two years after our separation, Riza's wife's father became ill, and she returned to Egypt. While she was in Egypt, Riza married an African sister; additionally, the doctors diagnosed him with prostate cancer; also, he and his African wife separated.

Many people were shocked that he had prostate cancer since he was a chiropractor and health conscious.

Riza tolerated his cancer well for about ten years, then it escalated. He was hospitalized for short periods, and believers rotated caring for him at his home under the supervision of Sister J. Waheeda and her husband, Brother Oliver. I cared for him several times, and he asked me to cook some soup for him which I made in the past.

I visited him twice or more at the Veteran's Hospital in West LA. On one of those occasions, when I was leaving, he told me that he loved me, but I did not respond.

Riza spent the last three or four weeks in a Veteran's Hospice facility in Westwood, California. The day before he expired, Saudia said we needed to visit him the next day to let him know we forgave him, and we did; he passed away shortly afterward.

Riza's last living sister, her daughter, his son, Kenneth, Saudia, I, and other believers attended the service.

May Allah bless him for teaching many people the Arabic language and may Allah accept his honorable deeds.

Chapter 15
My Extended Family

I started my manuscript by talking about the paternal side of my family, Laura, and Calvin Jordan, and their twelve children.

I already talked about my father, who married early and began moving north from Mississippi for a better life for himself and his family. My father's youngest brother, Uncle Love, followed him; but a few of my father's siblings remained in Mississippi their entire lives.

I knew Uncle Love's children from his second wife, Aunt Alice, because he and my father lived in Chicago. I also became familiar with Uncle Leland's adult children, my first cousins who migrated to Chicago from the South. I met many of my first and second cousins at the Jordan family reunions, which started about 45 years ago with Uncle Leland's daughter, Luella's son, Augustus, and two daughters in Mississippi. Uncle Leland's son, Leland Junior assisted Louella and her family.

Several years later, my first cousin, Hattie Evans, Uncle Lovelace's daughter, and his other children who lived in the Chicago area, and my father, Calvin, and his children had a reunion in the Chicago area.

Later, other Jordan Family members began having reunions in their areas. For example, Aunt Willie Jordan Shipp and her offspring had reunions in Ruleville, Mississippi; then, Ms. Vera Jordan Howze, a member of Uncle Leland's family, had their reunion in Cleveland, Mississippi.

Then, the Jordans' second and third generation decided to have one annual reunion in the states where the Jordan family resided. Since we started, Jordan family members have sponsored reunions annually in one of the following states: Mississippi, Illinois, Michigan, Ohio, Georgia, Florida, Missouri, California, and Tennessee. I love them.

The family reunion normally is the second week in July, and my vacation started the last of June. I did not want to go that far away for a weekend. Furthermore, I have siblings and other relatives in Chicago that I wanted to visit.

I called my cousin Hattie in Chicago, the president of the Chicago branch of the Jordan family reunion and explained my situation. She presented the issue to the members who changed the date. Therefore, I started attending reunions in the late 1980s.

My first family reunion was in Chicago, Illinois, at a church my family members frequented. After entering, I looked around for someone familiar to me but did not see anyone. Finally, I saw a young man who looked like my oldest nephew; hence, I went to him, introduced myself and told him he looked exactly like my oldest nephew, my father's grandson.

His name was Ellis Jordan, whose father was my first cousin, and his grandfather, Leland Jordan, was my father's older brother and my uncle. Ellis is my father's brother, Uncle Leland's, grandson. My father's grandson, William Graham, and my

149

father's brother, Leland's grandson, Ellis, strongly resemble each other.

I attended the family reunion in Toledo, Ohio several times; my most recent visit was in July 2019. The Toledo family members have a large church with a dining room downstairs. Quite a few of my cousins are ministers. At one of our reunions, one minister's sermon was Jonah in the Belly of the Whale, which I found interesting. Most of the cities I visited had pastors who were Jordan family members.

I got to know Ellis and his family well because we attended many family reunions in the same states.

My father, his youngest brother, Uncle Love, three of Uncle Leland's sons, and one of Uncle Leland's granddaughters, Gladys-Emma, migrated to Chicago and other states in the Midwest. Additionally, Aunt Willie's daughter, Marguerite, my first cousin moved from Mississippi to Chicago, then to Los Angeles. The majority of my first cousins that I knew were Uncle Love's and Uncle Leland's children. Some of my first cousins, born in the early 1880s, were deceased before I was born. So, I met my second and third cousins.

My first cousin, Loveless, and Louise Jordan and their family moved from Mississippi to Chicago, and later moved to Michigan. When Loveless and his family lived in Chicago, my sister Beatrice babysat for him and his wife.

I met his son, Melvin Jordan, my second cousin, at a family reunion in Chicago when he was married with children. We had a brief chat, and he told me they caravanned to the family reunion until they had an automobile accident and some of their children were injured. After the accident, they came via chartered bus.

Most of Uncle Leland's grandchildren currently living in Michigan are the children of his deceased children. I think of them as a close-knit group devoted to each other. They are excellent cooks, and each prepares a special dish, fried chicken, potato salad, peach cobblers, and more. I looked forward to their family reunions.

Uncle Leland's sons, Leland Junior, Loveless, Edward Shole Jordan, and Uncle Leland's granddaughter, Gladys, moved to Chicago.

I wrote earlier about my cousin, Edward Jordan, and his family, whom I frequently saw at our reunions and other family events. Doris, his wife, was loving and caring and would take everyone's children to her home. She and her family also cared for my mother when she aged.

Doris left us on December 23, 2011, and Edward remained with us until February 24, 2016. May G-d accept all their honorable deeds, caring for my mother, and reunite them in Paradise on the Day of Judgment to dwell there forever.

Hattie

My first cousin, Hattie, is also like an older sister. When we were young, we lived close to each other, and I walked to their house to play with her younger sister, Evelyn. I even spent the night at Hattie's house when she became an adult. My sister, Beatrice, lived with her sometimes. Although I knew her older and younger sister, I bonded with her.

Hattie has two daughters, one son, one granddaughter, and one great-granddaughter. Her oldest daughter, Alice, is a reverend who gave an entertaining sermon at the 2005 family reunion in Los Angeles.

At one of our family reunions, her granddaughter, Christelle, told me she sat on rural African American Mississippian residents' front porches and obtained information about the Jordan family while working on her master's degree. Christelle assisted Cheryl Vaughn, Aunt Willie's great-granddaughter, with the Jordan family tree.

Christelle was highly active in the church at an early age; later, she received a master's degree in divinity and traveled overseas. The last time I saw Christelle was at the 2018 family reunion. She told me she believed she was getting closer to finding information about Calvin and Laura's daughter, Lena. Unfortunately, Christelle passed away unexpectedly on December 2, 2021. I pray that G-d accepts her virtuous deeds, blots out any shortcomings, and reunites her in Paradise with all her family members on the Day of Judgment. AMEEN.

Phillip and James

Two of Uncle Love's youngest sons, Phillip, and James were close in age to my brother Calvin. All three of them married, had children, and remained friends until the end. Calvin lost his lifelong friends, but he is still alive.

Evelyn and Family

Evelyn was another one of Uncle Love's children and my childhood friend. She was very spiritual, but most of Uncle Love's children were because he was a preacher. She had at least four daughters and several sons; I knew most of her daughters. Evelyn married and shortly after, I got married. I moved to California, and we only saw each other at family reunions or other family events. Her daughter, Pam, and I had brief conversations when we saw each other. My nephew, Clarence, has known her daughter, Monica, since she was a small child. I do not remember seeing her sons, but Evelyn talked about them.

Evelyn passed away, and I miss seeing her at family reunions. May G-d bless her.

Lovey Lee and Family

After moving from Chicago, I only saw Lovey when I visited Chicago or at the family reunion, and she came to most of them. She has seven children and some grandchildren.

The last family reunion Lovie and I attended was in July 2014. She told me she did not know whether she was coming until her daughter and son-in-law decided to come. I am happy that I saw her because she passed away in October 2014. May G-d grant her and her family Paradise.

I met Lovie's daughter, Sandra, at the 2005 family reunion in Los Angeles, California, the first reunion held in California. Sandra could see that I was overwhelmed and immediately asked me whether I needed help. Of course, I said yes. She is very caring, and whenever she comes to a family reunion, she always volunteers to help in any way she can. She came to California early for the 2018 family reunion and assisted us.

Sandra is a widower with twin sons; one has three daughters. We were at the 2019 family reunion in Toledo, Ohio, the last one we attended since the Pandemic shut us down, and we had an enjoyable time.

Mary Ann and Family

Mary Ann and her late husband had several children and some grandchildren. She was cheerful and gave everyone a warm hug.

I know one of her daughters, Annette, her daughter's husband, Gregg, the outstanding family photographer, and her two adult children.

Her daughter, Myra, interviewed with the University of Southern California and the University of Chicago medical schools. She selected the University of Chicago, which is closer to home.

Her grandmother, Mary Ann, and the family were proud when Myra put on her white medical jacket.

Lovie and Mary Ann were remarkably close and did many things together; their daughters, Sandra, and Annette, are also perfect friends.

Since none of my siblings attended the 2019 family reunion, I enjoyed sharing a room with Mary Anne, which I will cherish because she passed away in March 2020. May G-d accept her honorable deeds and grant her and her family Paradise.

Gladys and Family

My Uncle Leland had one daughter, Louella, my first cousin, who married Mr. Edward, and they had one son, Augusta, who was the oldest, and two daughters, Gladys-Emma, and Verline. Augusta married Geraldine, and they had three children: one son and two daughters. Gladys-Emma and her spouse, Richard, had six children; Verline and her husband had four children. All of them are grand and great-grand parents.

I am sure I saw Augusta at least once, but I have seen his son, Donald, and his beautiful wife at several family reunions. He is very friendly, and we exchanged contact information. After our formal introduction, we had brief chats when we saw each other at the family reunion. One of my favorite second cousins was his aunt Gladys.

Augusta was interested in politics and instrumental in helping a lady, Ann Lanford, become the first Afro-American female elected council member in Chicago.

Augusta passed away in 1990. May G-d bless him for helping others to elevate in the political world. May G-d bless him for his honorable deeds and grant him paradise.

As previously stated, my brother Calvin and I went to Mississippi in 1954, so Calvin could assist our cousin, Eddie, to drive his children back to Chicago after spending a summer in Mississippi with their maternal grandparent. I went because I had never been to Mississippi, and that is when I met Emma-Gladys and her family.

Gladys got married in 1959 and moved to Chicago. I saw her occasionally when I visited Chicago. She was always affectionate and caring. When she saw me, she gave me a big hug, and told me she loved me.

According to her family, she was a great homemaker, seamstress, and gifted vocalist, which she transferred to her daughters. She also played basketball and passed the skills to her sons.

Gladys also had a sense of humor. Her oldest daughter left a six-figure position to become a reverend. Although she was proud of her daughter being a reverend, the six-figure position was also good.

Of course, I cannot omit Gladys, the businessperson who rapidly climbed the ranks of the Tupperware Organization. She managed a sales force and earned recognition for frequently exceeding all sales goals. In addition, her family was extremely pleased with her for the vacations she received as special sale awards which she shared with her family.

In March 2014, Gladys' son, Brig. General Ron Lewis, was selected to serve as the U.S. Army's Chief of Public Affairs at the Office of the Chief of Public Affairs in the Pentagon. What an outstanding achievement!

I called Gladys when she was not in good health. Unfortunately, she left us in April 2017. We all miss her caring, warmth, and smile.

May G-d accept her many honorable deeds, blot out any shortcomings she might have had, and reunite her with all her family in Paradise on the Day of Judgment.

Discovered a New Cousin in Los Angeles

My first cousin, Hattie in Chicago, who connected as many family members as possible, told me we had a second cousin, Louella, in Los Angeles. Hattie gave me Louella's contact information, and we connected.

Louella's father was my first cousin and one of my Uncle Leland's sons. She is the youngest of three children. Louella and her siblings have lived in Los Angeles since childhood, and both parents are deceased.

I met her brother, Alexander, Jr.; however, I never met her sister, who is now deceased. Louella is a paralegal, no longer married, and has four sons and grandchildren.

Chapter 16
My Grandchildren

Aishah

Saudia and her husband, Clinton Sutherland, gave me a granddaughter, Aishah, on August 18, 1990. She was gorgeous, with a patch of gray hair on her forehead. What a joyous day for me.

I was so excited about her that I almost canceled my annual conference trip to Atlanta, Georgia, via Ruleville, Mississippi, to see my elderly aunt, my father's youngest sister, and the last sibling in that family. However, I went.

Aishah, like most children, grew rapidly. As a young child, she did not like people ignoring her, and she stood by a person until the person acknowledged her, then she cheerfully left. Her father is seven feet tall and played basketball when he was younger.

I was eager to hear her talk, and whenever she said something incorrectly, I repeated it correctly. She would look at me to say, "you know what I said." She was always excited when she asked me whether I remembered something we had done previously, and I said yes; she walked or skipped away cheerfully.

When she was eight years old, Aishah played basketball in a private elementary school and a YMCA in Riverside, California, where her father taught. She also attended middle school and Santiago and Perris High Schools in California, graduating from

Perris High School. She was a talented player, with 6ft 2in proportions.

Time went by quickly, and the 11th grade arrived; therefore, she needed to consider selecting a college. Aishah performed well during high school; consequently, invitations were not a concern for her.

She got the most invitations from the University of Riverside in Riverside, California, located right in her backyard, and numerous more. Finally, she selected KU, Kansas University in Lawrence, Kansas, a quaint little hilly town I love, except for the chilly weather; but Aishah tolerated the weather for four years.

She received a full scholarship; as a result, she started classes in June 2008. The Jordan family reunion was in Missouri that year; hence, I spent several days on campus to monitor her conduct. Quite a learning experience.

Aishah's mother and I visited her on two other occasions at KU, including her graduation. When she walked down the streets or went into stores, you often heard, "Hi Aishah, great game." She was well known and admired.

In her senior year, she assisted the team in defeating Oklahoma State for the first time since 1981 with twenty rebounds and pulled down twenty-two boards, giving Oklahoma State its first home loss.

Only 14 Kansas University female basketball players in history reached 1500 + career points and 1,000 rebounds.

We are grateful for a cousin, La Shandra, who lives in Missouri, close to KU, who attended and took friends to Aishah's games, and our cousins in Ypsilanti, Michigan, who attended her Michigan game.

Aishah attended the KU 2012 summer session to complete her graduation requirements, then trained at the Atlanta Dream team for several weeks and played one game before traveling overseas. With the exception of one year since graduating from Kansas University in 2012, Aishah has played professional basketball in the countries listed below for one or two consecutive basketball seasons.

- Italy
- Poland - 2014, 2021, and 2022
- Latvia
- Lebanon - One Summer
- Spain - three months
- South Korea - twice
- Israel - one month
- Poland 2021-2022 season

Shereen

Shereen, my second granddaughter, loved affection. Aishah talked early, but Shereen did not talk. Even though I was eager to hear her talk, she did not talk until she was about two and a half or three years old.

One day something happened, and she said, "How incredible!" I was awed. She had a voice, and she loved to sing. She sang at many events while attending nursery, preschool, and kindergarten when she was young. However, she was no longer interested in singing when she became older.

Shereen began participating in sports in middle school, and played volleyball, golf, tennis, and track; Aishah only played basketball.

Shereen attended La Sierra High School for her first two years and played basketball, volleyball, and track. Her last two years were at Santiago High School, where she played the same sports as she did at La Sierra; she graduated in 2012.

In 2012, Shereen got a full scholarship to the University of Arizona; however, she transferred to the University of California, Irvine, after one and one-half years.

She graduated from UC Irvine on June 16, 2017. She played in a basketball tournament in China for one month, then played basketball overseas. She spent the past five years playing professional basketball in Switzerland, England, Sweden, France, Romania, Turkey, and Germany.

Furthermore, she is currently taking online college classes to further her education.

Chapter 17
Masjid Omar Ibn al-KhattAb

After Riza and I departed, I was looking for a change and began attending Masjid Omar Ibn al-Khattab. Masjid Omar Ibn Khattab is a beautiful, peaceful place of worship, especially for an individual who needs a change. Moreover, I did not know many people, and *few of them knew me;* but I did not have "pity parties."

The location of the masjid is in the area where I worked, so I saw the workers building the masjid until they completed the structure. I looked forward to visiting the masjid when it was complete. One of my coworkers and I attended the opening service, and we enjoyed the presentation and the roasted lamb and rice immensely.

I attended the masjid for Friday prayer and Sunday Islamic studies class and became familiar with the administrators.

A Muslim sister from overseas, now deceased, funded the construction of Masjid Omar so the students who attend USC (The University of Southern California), located three blocks north of Omar, could have a place close to USC to attend for prayer.

Her son, Dafer Dakhil, one of the masjid's administrators, planned the facility's activities, including banquets and honorary events. I was fortunate to be invited to some of them.

After the passing of his mother, Dafer's father remained in California and visited Masjid Omar and his home overseas until he passed away. To my knowledge, Dafer's brothers, sisters, and their families still live in the California area.

In the mid-nineties, Dafer and his wife had two school-age children, and he was passionate about education and supportive of educators. So, he invited some educators to *An Evening for Educators* in May 1998 in the banquet hall. Of course, we had an excellent meal and received "Islam in the Curriculum" to supplement our basic educational materials.

One weekend, his wife, an excellent cook, assisted a group of teachers in cooking mid-eastern food. We cooked more than six entrees, including baklava. Later, I prepared many of the recipes at home, and they were delicious.

I knew two sisters who took the classes, Judy Moussa and Abrafi Sanyika. Occasionally, Judy hosted gatherings in her gorgeous, spacious Jefferson Park home until she returned to her home in Detroit. Now she sponsors a Zoom meeting twice per month on Sunday, discussing topics on Al Islam. She also has guest speakers.

The other sister Abrafi is a worldwide traveler and publisher writing her second book. She is exciting and truly knowledgeable. We talked about her trips, and she told me that the best trip she made was to the Hajj in Mecca. She also traveled to West Africa, Ghana, and Timbuktu.

Chapter 18
The Month of Ramadan

Ramadan, the ninth month of the Muslim lunar year, is a significant event for Muslims. We fast for 29 or 30 days from dusk to dawn, endeavor to read the entire Quran, and complete other rituals. Masjid Omar had banquets during Ramadan, and I was fortunate to attend some of them. The attendees, especially the females, were always eloquently dressed, and the food was delicious.

I enjoyed the recitation of the Holy Quran by the guest speakers from middle eastern countries. each night, the imam reads one and one-fourths of the Quran to complete the entire book within 29 days. In addition, two biological sisters from Ethiopia, who were fluent in Arabic, assisted me following the recitation.

One young brother, Mustafa, from Turkey, was fluent in English and several other languages; he taped the Holy Quran simultaneously with the English translation, making it easier for English speakers to follow. When I heard verses repeated frequently that I thought were significant, I wrote them down and looked them up later at home, which increased my Arabic vocabulary.

Muslims are required to make five daily prayers. However, during Ramadan, we can make Tarawih Prayer 3, a Sunnah prayer performed by Prophet Muhammad (ﷺ), after the Isha'a prayer.

Shaf' and Witr prayers start after Isha prayer and should be completed before the time of Fajr prayer. Shaf' is two rak'ah, and Witr is one. Prophet Muhammad (may the peace and blessings be upon him) said, "Make Witr your last prayer at night." [4]

Night of Power

Many believers attend the Night of Power during the last ten days of Ramadan. Some remain all night and nap before performing the Tahajjud prayer between midnight and dawn. It is the night that some Imams complete the reading of the Holy Quran at the masjid. Those who had not finished reading the Quran try to complete the book that night because of the blessings they receive.

I recall a particular Night of Power; the sermon was spiritually uplifting.

The sermon was in Arabic; therefore, I did not understand most of the speech; however, I knew it must have been significant because many immigrant sisters were crying; consequently, I joined them. When I read the English translation of the sermon, my assumption was correct.

Chapter 19
Islamic Scholars Who Have
Influenced My Life

Brother Mu'min

Sister Ameerah, the teacher I wrote about earlier, told me about an Islamic study class on Sunday mornings at Masjid Omar, so I started attending the class with some other brothers and sisters. Initially, Doctor Yahia Abdul-Rahman taught the course; however, Brother Mu'min, a knowledgeable, patient, generous brother, became the permanent instructor. Besides being well versed in the Quran, his explanation of the Quran was clear.

Brother Mu'min's wife was a healthcare provider. They have four adult children, two sons and two daughters, all professionals, scientists, medical doctors, and dentists. Brother Mu'min and his wife also have grandchildren.

Brother Mu'min taught the class from the late 1990s to about 2015, and Sister Raheemah and I remained in the class until he became ill. Unfortunately, he succumbed to his illness. The class members miss him, and we pray that Allah grants him the highest place in Paradise for his devotion to helping believers learn Al Islam.

Brother Talib, a younger brother from Lebanon, assisted Brother Mu'min occasionally. He is an engineer and works in Los

Angeles. He is married and has two young adult children and two almost adult children. We enjoyed having him.

Sheik Ahmed Karamate, from Turkey, Resident Imam at Masjid Omar, asked Brother Mu'min whether anyone in his Islamic study class was interested in learning Arabic after his session. He taught those of us who were interested in short Ayat's (short paragraphs in the Quran) and surahs from the Quran for many years.

Sheik Karamate and his son Mustafa and Mustafa's family returned to Turkey in 2010. The class members missed all of them. Sheik Karamate passed away. May Allah bless and grant him Paradise, and may Allah comfort Mustafa, his wife, and children for their loss.

We have another well-qualified Islamic Studies instructor, whom we appreciate, Imam Hafiz, who spent eight years in Saudi Arabia with his wife, Sister Sofia, studying the Quran and Al Islam.

Dr. Yahia Abdul-Rahman

Many brothers do the Friday Jumu'ah Prayer Lecture; however, I heard Dr. Yahia speak many times. There were several comments he made that still resonate with me. First, he said, sometimes things happen to us, and we think that is the worst thing that could happen to us, but it turns out to be good for us. I found that statement to be true.

Also, he stated if married brothers assume additional wives, their children would not be pleased with their fathers hurting their mothers. I believe that to be a profound statement.

In one of his Friday sermons, he stated that reciting the Quran is the best way to celebrate it. This sermon might have been a khutbah during Ramadan because he gave us a list of things to do during Ramadan, which included:

1. Praying.
2. Come to Tarawih prayer and bring our children with us.
3. Invite Muslims to the masjid.
4. Visit the ill.
5. Mend any misunderstandings.
6. Pay zakat.

He also told us to take notes of the Jummah meetings. May Allah bless him for all his honorable deeds. I have not seen him recently due to the pandemic, but inshallah, I hope he is well, and I might see him again.

Dr. Hassan Hathout

I was impressed by Dr. Hassan Hathout's concern for resolving the conflict in the Middle East. I heard him speak several times on that and other topics.

He was a medical physician, and I read he was a Southern California Islamic community leader. He was the head of efforts to simplify American Muslims and build interfaith bonds.

Additionally, he was the leader of the Islamic Center of Southern California, where he coordinated outreach for two decades. He was a renowned scholar who authored several books, one, *Reading the Muslim Mind*, which was well worth reading.

In 1998, Dr. Hassan delivered the first White House celebration of Eid Al Fitrah at the end of the Muslim's holy month of Ramadan.

Dr. Hassan is no longer with us. May Allah grant him the highest place in Paradise for his many years of arduous work in the advancement of Al Islam.

Dr. Ahmad Sakr

I also heard Dr. Ahmad Sakr, a Ph.D., speak about his admiration for the late Imam Warithuddin Muhammad at a Sunday gathering at Masjid Omar. Additionally, I heard several of his Friday Khutbahs.

Dr. Sakr was a founding member of the World Council of Mosques, whose headquarters are in Makkah. He was the first director and representative of the Muslim World League to the UN in New York and the Foundation for Islamic Knowledge president. He was active in other organizations.

Some books he wrote are *Understanding Islam* and *Muslims and Family Values in Islam*. He also wrote a Tafseer on Surah Al-Fatiha. Additionally, here are a few topics that Dr. Sakr wrote about in some of his books and booklets: Islam, food, health, behavior, terrorism, fundamentalism, Khutab, and orations. His wish was to build a bridge of understanding through commonalities between Muslims and non-Muslims.

Although he is no longer with us, May Allah bless him for his endeavor to enlighten people on Allah, Al Islam, behavior, and many other topics.

Dr. Fathi Osman

Dr. Fathi Osman is another Islamic scholar who has published more than twenty-five books in Arabic and English. I heard him speak at several Friday Jummah prayer services, and he published a book, *Concepts of the Quran*, which I purchased and hope to read soon.

I cannot conclude my talk about the many people that I encountered at Masjid Omar Ibn Al-Khattab without thanking

Brother Abdullah, the manager of the facility, who ensures that the Masjid is well maintained.

The End of 1995 to the Beginning of 2000

Chapter 20
The Accidents

In August 1995, I received a call at work telling me my daughter was in an automobile accident and I needed to go to Riverside California Hospital immediately. I notified the school office that I had an emergency and needed a replacement.

I did not know the severity of the accident until I arrived at the hospital; therefore, as I drove, I prayed to Allah that her injuries were minor. By the time I arrived, I was emotionally distressed, compounded by the clerical staff's inability to locate her promptly. Alhamdulillah, (praise be to G-d) her injuries were not life-threatening, but she needed surgery and blood, and I gave her blood.

The surgery was successful, but the doctor told her that she would need a hip replacement at an early age, and she did, which was also successful.

When Saudia's husband finished work, he picked up the children from Saudia's friend, Mitzi, and brought them home. I cooked, fed, and bathed, then put them to bed. After driving sixty miles from Los Angeles to Riverside and doing other chores, I was exhausted, so I showered, ate, and went to bed.

Fortunately, it was close to summer break for me; therefore, I was able to spend several weeks with Saudia when she returned home. Allah is Merciful.

Until I reached my seventies, I seldom had colds or the annual flu; after I became seventy, things changed. First, I had hip replacement surgery in 2007, then diverticulosis, which required minor surgery, and back surgeries in 2012 and 2021. In 2015, I had glaucoma surgery on both eyes; in 2016, I had cataract surgery. I also broke my right foot at home while walking down the stairs.

Then, I had two automobile accidents, one on October 29, 2015, and the second on April 27, 2019. The most serious accident happened on October 29, 2015, in a 2003 Subaru Baja. When I was ready to drive my car into the garage, I noticed that my left rear-view mirror was too close to the door. Therefore, I put my foot on the brake and put the car in reverse. The vehicle went backward and forward several times, then hit the left side of the fence, turned around, and stopped. I sat there stunned and traumatized and thanked Allah that I was not in traffic; otherwise, it could have been a fatal accident. Praise be to Allah. I am still walking, albeit slowly.

Chapter 21
Traveling

Sister Mahasin Shamsiddeen was my traveling partner, and we traveled far and near, from Los Angeles to New Jersey, New York, Las Vegas, Nevada, Oakland, California, and more.

Mahasin, Joan Sabree, Elaine Saafir, and I attended several functions at the masjid in Garden Grove, about twenty-five miles from Los Angeles. The sisters made and sold Islamic garments, or a person could purchase their fabric and have their item made, which is what I did.

The sisters also prepared delicious lunches, and a halal market with meat, fruit, and vegetables was near.

Sister Elaine and I traveled to one of Imam Muhammad's conventions in Louisville, Kentucky, which was her first time making an airline reservation. We had an enjoyable all-day ride with several stops and changes in planes. But our suite was spacious and comfortable, and Imam Muhammad's speech spiritually enlightening.

Several of us attended Oakland's Annual Evening of Elegance, which included a fashion show on Saturday night and the sisters' breakfast on Sunday morning. The event was always enjoyable.

We stayed in non-gambling hotels in Las Vegas. The three-day weekend activities were at the masjid with lots of delicious food, tours, and entertainment. I enjoyed those trips.

Mahasin, Joan Sabree, and I went to an annual Islamic convention in New Jersey, where Imam Muhammad was the keynote speaker. I shared a room with Sister Joan, and when she returned to the room, she told me that Princess Diana had passed away in an automobile accident. The news was shocking and sad.

We took a three-day trip to San Diego one weekend, joined by a special guest, Sister Ayesha Mustafa from the Muslim Journal. We took our sleeping bags, slept in the masjid, and cooked our food. Among other things, we discussed Islamic female issues.

The sisters took us on a city tour, and then we went to Sister Brenda Saafir's home before returning to the masjid.

Sister Elaine and I went to one of Imam Muhammad's presentations in Fresno, California.

Imam Muhammad made two more trips to San Diego. On one of those trips, he demonstrated the correct procedure to slaughter an animal to make it halal.

Imam Muhammad returned in March 2003 for Imam Ali Rasheed of New York's (formerly Captain Edward 2X of Los Angeles) "Posthumous" Appreciation Tribute Banquet. His last visit to California was San Diego in April 2008 for a Saturday night banquet and a Sunday afternoon Taaleem service.

Sisters Joan Sabree, along several other sisters and I, went to Bakersfield, California to participate in an event where Imam Muhammed was to be the keynote speaker. On that occasion, we drove. On our second trip, we took the train from Los Angeles to Bakersfield to see Imam Yusuf Islam and his lovely wife, Sister Daaiyah's newly built, gorgeous, spacious home. The food was even better, and we had a restful return home.

Imam Yusuf and Sister Daaiyah are no longer with us. I pray that Allah accepts their honorable deeds and Imam Islam's effort to spread Islam in the Bakersfield area and grant them both Paradise.

Chapter 22
Former College Classmates, Colleagues, and Others

Sharron Daniels

Sharron Daniels, Pecolia McFarland, several other students, and I attended California State University, Los Angeles, in the late sixties. Pecolia and I taught at the same high school until I retired in 1999 and remained in contact until she expired December 2014. I enjoyed conversing with her, and I miss her.

Sharron and I met in the late 1960s at California State University in the Teachers' Training class. During that period, many minority students became teachers because tuition was low, and we only had to purchase textbooks, notebooks, and other supplies.

After completing our requirements, minority teachers immediately found work in South Central and East Los Angeles. But I worked at a private school and a skill center while acquiring my master's degree and completing my teaching credentials, then I taught for the Los Angeles Unified School District for 19 years full-time and five years part-time and retired.

Sharron was an excellent instructor who taught at Markham Middle School for many years until she transferred to Fremont High School and remained there until she retired. She received several outstanding teachers' awards.

Sharron was the only girl in her family with one or two brothers; she and her mother were close. After completing college, she married and had one son, who became a doctor. Her son had a daughter who was the light of Sharron's life.

After her mother's death, she traveled to some African countries and throughout the United States. We occasionally talk about our grandchildren and other exciting things happening in our lives. Hopefully, we will remain in contact.

Georgia Pettis

Georgia Pettis, my former coworker who replaced a teacher at Manual Arts High School in 1997, is a reliable, dependable, outspoken friend. When I met her, she was a divorced mother with two adult sons; now, she has three grandchildren and one adorable great-grandson. Her grandson, Kendall Michael Pettis is an outstanding Oklahoma University Sooner baseball player.

Georgia loves to cook and is an excellent cook and baker. She invites relatives and friends to meals for various occasions; her coconut cakes, pound cakes, peach cobblers, and pecan pies are outstanding.

She has a friend, Rick, who does maintenance work and helps me with repairs when needed. In July 2018, I went to a family reunion in Toledo, Ohio; and I wanted to stop in Detroit, Michigan, which is about thirty-five miles away, to visit a critically ill hospitalized friend.

The best flight would make me arrive in Detroit before 6:00 am, and that was before visitation hours; therefore, I would need to stay in a hotel for several hours, get transportation to the hospital to see my friend, then go to Toledo. What a chore!

Unfortunately, my friend expired on July 4, 2019, and the family reunion was the following week.

Rick to the Rescue

I remembered Rick talking about his nieces in Detroit, so I asked Georgia to call Rick to see whether I could stay with one of his nieces for several hours before going to Toledo, Ohio. Not only did his niece pick me up from the airport and take me to her house to search and secure ground transportation to Toledo, but she drove me to the hotel in Toledo when she was unable to find transportation and I had to force money on her. What a blessing!

Saundra, My Cosmetologist Sister-Friend

A fellow teacher, Phyllis's hair was always well groomed and grew rapidly; hence, I had to know her cosmetologist. She told me, Saundra Hightower, and she said it takes a long time to get an appointment with her. She was right because it took me a year to get an appointment.

Saundra was a traveling stylist, and when she came to my home, she greeted me warmly as though she had known me forever. When I met her in 1986, she was married and had three children, two teenagers (male and female), and one friendly little girl, who came with her when school was out.

Saundra was from a large family; her parents were still living when I met her, and her father owned a mom-and-pop store. She had one sister and several brothers; she and her mother were close.

Saundra was gregarious and deeply knowledgeable. We talked about daily events and the nightly news; she enjoyed eating, and I cooked.

Saundra was versatile by using different techniques during the year, including braids, pressing, or perms, and the result was long hair. When she braided your hair, that was usually a weekend job.

In the mid-1990s, an Afro-American female created a unique technique using several small tools to style Afro-American hair without heat or perm, and the business snowballed. She trained cosmetologists to become Sisterloc Consultants in a brief period, with minimum fees. A friend who had Sisterlocs convinced me to get them, and I still have them. Later, Saundra took the training and became my Sisterloc's consultant.

Since 2018, Saundra has not been able to do Sisterlocs. Also, she lost her father, only son, and other relatives some years ago. Her daughters and sons-in-law have blessed her with seven grandchildren and seven plus great-grandchildren. She lost her beloved, 97-year-old, mother on May 18, 2022, but she remains strong, and we still talk. May G-d continue to bless her.

I had three Sisterloc consultants before Saundra. I do not remember the name of the consultant who initially locked my hair, but the other two are Mrs. Barbara Bramwell and Sister Baseemah; both did an excellent job.

Retirement

I filled my days after retirement with many new activities.

One of my former colleagues told me that the Los Angeles Unified School District was giving incentives to teachers who retired in 1999, so I decided to investigate and thought it would benefit me.

I had just completed a class on how to write a business plan because I wanted to make dolls using my youngest granddaughter's face. Initially, I needed to find a school near me that taught the creation of doll faces. I found one near Santa Barbara. I knew several of Elaine Saafir's sons attended or graduated from Fresno State University; therefore, I asked her for directions; instead, she offered to help me drive. I did not want to go alone, but I disliked imposing myself on people. I said yes immediately.

We had an enjoyable weekend. Elaine is athletic, so she spent her weekend riding bicycles and exercising while I learned to create a doll face. May Allah bless her for helping me to feel secure.

Even though I did not make the dolls, I accomplished many other goals. I wanted to teach in a community college before my teaching career ended. My neighbor, Dr. Jacquelyn Scott, who enjoyed helping people, taught at several community colleges and assisted me in getting a part-time position at a community college.

Additionally, my dear sister and friend, Asilah, knew I would not sit at home all day idle. Therefore, she asked her neighbor, a homeschool teacher, for contact information for homeschooling, and I became a homeschool teacher for five years.

Chapter 23
My Other Supporters

Joan Sabree-Faqir

I met Joan when she moved to Los Angeles, California. She was articulate and passionate about education and worked at colleges in some of the southern states and Sister Clara Muhammad Schools in various states, including Los Angeles, California.

Sister Joan started a non-profit organization, Al Taliah, "Vanguards for Literacy," which focused on activities to support and fund literature to enhance education and cultural enrichment with the help of the supporters listed below.

Al Taliah Supporters

- Khalid Abdul Muqaddim and his wife
- Garth Abdur Raqeeb and his mother
- Omar Rushdan
- Janice Haqq
- J Waheeda
- Jackie G
- Karen English
- Rose
- Daaimah (me)
- Freeda

The educational part was designed to support the literacy of individuals of all ages. Additionally, Al Taliah sponsored group field trips to Allensworth State Park, Catalina Island, The California African American Museum, and more. Al Taliah also had fundraising events for the Center for Advanced Learning (CAL), the Islah LA Academy, and book drives for the children's Eid Celebration gifts.

Joan enjoyed traveling and for several years served as the West Coast Correspondent for the Muslim Journal; the believers were pleased to receive the information.

Joan is no longer with us, but May Allah bless her for helping many children to achieve their educational goals. Sister Rose and Garth's mother are no longer with us; may Allah also bless them and grant them Paradise.

Asilah, Again

I have known Asilah Shakoor since the 1980s, but I did not realize how she functions during an emergency. She is a registered nurse with advanced training and a massage therapist, married to Nelson El Amin, MD, who has supported her on many occasions. Both she and her husband have an adult son. Asilah also had two grandsons; unfortunately, one passed away in a vehicle accident.

One Friday after Jummah prayer, I stopped by the cleaners to pick up my suit for an out-of-state trip, later in the evening, to my friend's daughter's graduation from college in Minnesota. When I arrived home, I parked in the front, went upstairs only to find the lock on my door broken, and the door opened. The first person I thought about was Asilah; therefore, I sat in my car, called her, and waited until she arrived. She took me to a locksmith because she did not have his card, but she remembered his location. He came to the house and repaired the lock. That is just one of the many things she has done for me.

When she knows individuals or families in need, she collects funds for them from a group of believers. She is kindhearted and sympathetic to those who are less fortunate.

Asilah is known for taking people home from the masjid, regardless of how far they live. For months, she went to Skid Row and washed the homeless feet. On her first trip, she washed the feet of a believer who frequently attended masjid, Bilal Ibn Rabah. She is noble, and I pray that Allah continues to bless her.

There are a few believers that I knew, some of whom are no longer with us, that I would like to mention.

Sister Rashidah Akbar and Her Family

I saw Sister Rashidah in the 1970s at Temple #27 and later at the masjid. She was married and had two children, a daughter who was one of my students at the Sister Clara Muhammad School (aka) the University of Islam, and a younger son. Her children are both married with children.

Sister Rashidah and her husband, Brother Wali, were entertainers who wrote and sang Islamic songs, which most of us enjoyed. Sister Rashidah and I never engaged in lengthy conversation until the 1990s, when we discovered we had something in common: real estate. After Rashidah retired, we attended a real estate meeting on how to reduce a 30-year real estate mortgage.

The next time I saw her was at Jummah prayer, where she sold me a Muslim Journal paper, and we talked briefly. The following Tuesday morning, after Fajr prayer, I received a call from Sister Arnette telling me that Sister Rashidah had passed away earlier that morning, and I was shocked and saddened.

Four years after his wife passed away, Brother Wali married Sister Shahidah, and they remained married until he passed away in 2020; then, she returned to Missouri with her family.

May Allah bless Sister Shahidah for caring for and nourishing Brother Wali during his illness.

Sister Valeria Shaheed

Sister Valeria became a member of the Nation of Islam in 1973, then Al Islam in 1975. She married former Harlem Globetrotter William Garner in 1963, and they had a daughter, Carla Denise.

Sister Valeria helped to serve meals at many of the functions at the masjid, especially during Ramadan. May Allah bless her for her helpfulness.

Sister Rasheedah Adelah Hameed

Sister Rasheedah accepted Al Islam in 1978. She was the mother of three children, one of whom preceded her in death, and a registered nurse at County USC Hospital for seventeen years.

After working for 17 years as a nurse, she decided to use her creative talents to direct inner-city youth to keep them off the street and feature their acting skills. Sister Rasheedah also published a book.

She is no longer with us, but may Allah bless her efforts to raise the level of the inner-city youth.

Sister Shahidah Zakiyah Karim-Khalid aka, Denise Gipson

Sister Shahidah joined the Nation of Islam in Los Angeles in 1959, then worked as the secretary-treasurer at Temple #27 from 1977 until 1984. I met her shortly after I moved to Los Angeles in 1960, and I remembered her always having a smile.

In 1975, she started visiting prisons in Arizona, and in 1980 she began volunteering as a minister for women at Cybil Brand County Jail in Los Angeles.

In 1990, she was appointed the first female chaplain for the State of California Department of Corrections. She worked at California Institute for Women and California Rehabilitation Center for many years.

Sister Shahidah passed away in January 2020. May Allah bless her for the many women whose lives she helped to improve.

Sister Aneesah Rasheed and Sons

Aneesah moved to Los Angeles, California, in 1971 from Pontiac, Michigan, to increase the chances of her four sons' success in their future endeavors.

She worked for McDonald Douglas Aerospace Company.

She became a member of the Nation of Islam in Long Beach in 1973, later named Masjid Al-Shareef. She also attended Bilal Islamic Center and Bilal Ibn Rabah. Furthermore, she was an excellent seamstress who made garments for many sisters.

She enrolled her four sons in the University of Islam's School because she believed they could receive an equal education, which would increase their self-esteem. I am sure I met her when she enrolled her oldest son, Leon, in my class.

She was at various masjids for many years and assisted wherever needed.

Sister Aneesah is no longer with us. I pray Allah grants her Paradise and comforts her sons, grand, and great-grandchildren.

(Hajjah) Raheemah Hasan

Sister Raheemah Hasan, aka Curline Lewis, became a member of the Nation of Islam in 1965 in California and embraced Al Islam in 1975 in Los Angeles. She was married and had two sons and later some grandchildren. She worked in the aerospace industry for more than twenty years.

Allah blessed her to make Hajj. She is no longer with us; however, I pray that Allah accepts her honorable deeds and grants her Paradise.

Sister Lateefah Mustafa aka Valeria Andrews

Sister Lateefah and her husband and son became members of the Nation of Islam in Los Angeles, California, at Temple #27 in 1960. I met her shortly after moving to Los Angeles.

She attended Masjid Al-Shareef in Long Beach and participated in many of their social functions, especially with her friend Sister Kay.

Her husband repaired washing machines, including mine. The family is no longer here, but may Allah bless them with Paradise.

Sister Raheema Salaam aka Darlene Gibbs

Sister Raheema from Detroit, Michigan had two adult children, one male, and one female. She was a clean culinary art student, who owned a bakery in Los Angeles, and all her food was delicious.

She was a member and coordinator of the Quranic Study Class at Masjid Omar and made coffee and baked pastries for the class.

Allah blessed her to make Hajj, and inshallah may He grant her Paradise for all her honorable deeds. (AMEN)

Sister Minnie and Her Sons

I met Sister Minnie and her family lived in Los Angeles, California, andshe was my babysitter intermittently. Her youngest son, Wali, was my student. Wali and my daughter, Saudia, are close in age and attended the University of Islam School.

She was kind and caring, especially if a person needed to be consoled, which I did once, and she was there. Sister Minnie is no longer with us; however, I pray that Allah accepts her honorable deeds and kindness and grants her Paradise. Wali is doing well and attends the Sunday Quranic class.

Sister Helen

I must mention Sister Helen, who had a granddaughter close to my daughter's age, and was previously my babysitter. She did an excellent job. She is no longer with us, but may Allah accept her honorable deeds and grant her Paradise.

Doctors in Our Community

Dr. Khadijah Lang, MD is a Family Medicine Specialist in Los Angeles, CA, whom I visited several times. Her daughter, Qiyamah is designing the cover for my book.

Dr. Tawheed (Dr. Artice Terrel), a chiropractor, treated me for several automobile accidents. His treatments are relaxing.

Dr. Battle-Bey is an alternative MD, from whom I have had exceptionally satisfactory results.

Former President Barak Obama

I am among many people who never thought we would live to see a person of color the President of the United States of America; but we did, and I thank G-d. I frequently prayed to Allah (G-d) for his safety and that of his family.

I thank Mr. Obama for the accomplishments he achieved, despite the impediments he faced.

Mr. Obama and I have the same birth month, he and my daughter have the same birth year.

Imams

Ayman Abdul Mujeeb, aka Donald 27X, became a member of the Nation of Islam in 1973, then embraced Al-Islam in 1975, when Imam Warith Deen Muhammad became the leader of the Nation of Islam.

He was a young, energetic man ready to work; therefore, he rose to become the top seller of the *Muhammad Speaks* newspaper and the bean pies. Later, he became a member of the Whiting H&G team. Additionally, he learned Arabic proficiently enough to teach it to children and adults; besides, he was the first muezzin in California.

Coupled with his long-time friend and businessperson, Abdul-Rahim Muhammad, aka Thomas 17X, they propelled to unbelievable heights selling the fish, spreading Islam, and getting new converts.

Brother Rahim's daughter, Najah, told me that Imam Ayman and their families were inseparable.

Occasionally, I talked with Imam Ayman. He was interesting and told me I should write my life story, and now, I am. He became an Imam and replaced Imam Riza Khalillah, at Masjid Bilal ibn Rabah after his death.

Imam Ayman's wife, Sister Khadijah, a health care provider, and educator, has an annual event on health which includes a Friday night banquet with speakers from health care facilities.

On the Saturday morning following the event, we had a "Walk for Wellness" parade around the area near Masjid Bilal Ibn Rabah. Seniors who were unable to walk rode in buggies drawn by motor vehicles. Healthcare representatives from various facilities gave literature to the audience and vendors sold their products. We had plenty of delicious food and the event was productive for everyone.

Imam Ayman is no longer with us, and I pray that Allah blesses him with Paradise for his endeavors to uplift humanity. Brother Hateem Shareef, whose parents were members of the Nation of Islam when he was born, is now the Imam of Bilal Ibn Rabah.

Imam Abdul Karim Hasan has been the Minister, then Imam, in the Los Angeles area since 1972. Now he is the Imam of the newly opened masjid on King and Central Avenue. May Allah continue to bless him.

Someone told me there was a picture of my late husband, Ronald T. Stokes holding our daughter, Saudia, when she was an infant. I tried unsuccessfully to get some Believer to help me locate the picture. Then a sister, Janice Haqq told me there were some pictures in a trailer at Bilal Islamic Center on Central Avenue in Los Angeles, California.

Ronald was from the east coast, and Imam, Abdul Karim Hasan lived on the east coast prior to moving to Los Angeles; therefore, I called Imam Karim and asked him whether he could find someone on the east coast who had seen the picture. Imam explained that since that was sixty years ago, not very many people were still with us; he would try.

Imam Hasan called me several weeks later to tell me that he had found one brother, who needed additional information regarding Ronald, which I provided him with. About 7:20 pm on Saturday, December 31, 2022, I received a call from Imam Hasan who informed me that Brother Abdul Latif U.H. Muhammad from Charlotte, North Carolina, found the picture of Ronald holding Saudia in the 1962 archive located at The University of California, Northridge, less than thirty miles from where I live. Praise be to Allah the Most Merciful. Inshallah, I will be able to put the picture on the cover of my book.

Imam Saadiq Saafir was the Imam at Masjid Ibadillah in Jefferson Park for many years, then the Masjid moved to 2950 West Slauson, in Los Angeles. His son, Jihad, replaced him and he frequently talks about the times he looked at his father and felt pleased to have his father looking at him.

I still remember two things Imam Jihad taught us: a dua you can make in bed, and reminder to pray Ayat al-Kursi daily.

Thank you, continue the good works, and may Allah bless you.

Closing Remarks: My Hope

Primarily, I thank Allah for blessing me to complete this book. There were times when I almost quit, but with the help of Allah, Sister Muslima's technology skills, and Sister Elaine Saafir's superb language art skills, I am almost finished.

I spent many years in educational institutions achieving degrees, none of which I regret. However, I want to spend more time learning the Quran and Islam and improving my relationship with my daughter.

This book has been about expressing my gratitude, but I still want to thank a few more people:

My sincere thanks to Brother Aadil Naazir for his kindness in finding me seats at crowded events. Both of us taught at the University of Islam in the 1970s. May Allah's peace and blessings be upon him.

May Allah bless Brother Samee Samia, a long-standing member of Masjid Bilal-ibn Rabah, who conducts the Fajr and Isha'a prayers daily via telephone: what a blessing.

Sister Renee Mustafa and Sister Khadijah Diop are two of our excellent cooks in the Los Angeles area.

***

Now that you know a little bit about my personal family, my experience and my first-hand accounts with the Nation of Islam and Islam in America, my prayer is that you continue to study your own family history, your own spirituality and your own relationship to Allah.

Endnotes

1. Note, after 1933, my father's last name was changed from Jordan to Jardan by Fard Muhammad
2. My thanks to Sister Barbara's daughter, Priscilla, for most of the information about Sister Barbara's activities after the trauma at the temple on April 27th, 1962.
3. Tarawih prayer consists of eight rak'ahs, with salutations after every two rak'ahs.
4. Material from Imam Warithuddin Muhammad's book *Prayer and Al-Islam*.

About the Author

Delores Daaimah Jardan is a retired educator who dedicated her life to teaching and ensuring that students of all ethnic backgrounds receive an adequate education. She is a cornerstone in the religion of Islam among African Americans who converted to The Nation of Islam. She is very humble and compassionate about anything she touches.

Sr. Daaimah is well respected among the community and a strong believer in the One G-d (Allah). Her commitment to Al-Islam has earned respect from many diverse people and she has strong relationships with many different communities. Those who have encountered her are willing to assist in any way to ensure she is comfortable and not challenged with prolonged standing or walking when attending community activities, i.e., prayer, social activities, etc.

Sr. Daaimah consistently assists others in need and will offer them housing until they get on their feet.

Sr. Daaimah is a mother and grandmother. Many of her former students acknowledge her as a grandmother. She is well respected among the community and loves to move.

She hopes that her book will enlighten people all over the world!

MEMORIES

THE JARDANS

My Parents
Calvin & Georgia Jardan

Program from our Jordan Family Reunion in 2015

Aunt Matilda, my Uncle Leland's Wife's

Me and Saudia, my daughter, Circa 1964

Saudia

Saudia, with her husband Clinton Sutterland

My granddaughter, Aishah
(My daughter Saudia's Daughter)

My Granddaughter, Aishah

By Gary Bedore
gbedore@ljworld.com

It's probably fitting Kansas University's basketball team wrapped up — and celebrated — the program's eighth-straight Big 12 regular-season championship late Monday night at Oklahoma State.

According to ninth-year coach Bill Self ... it's the Jayhawks' performance on the road that's annually separated his squad from the rest of the pack.

"Winning at home is great. You always want to win at home. We have an advantage to winning at home because we have great players, an unbelievable building and fan support," said Self. His Jayhawks have compiled a 68-4 Big 12 record at home in the Self-era entering Saturday's 8 p.m. regular-season finale versus Texas.

"Somebody told me today we're 33-20 on the road in league play — 53-20 is pretty amazing," added Self, whose Jayhawks actually are 54-19 on the road. "We went 7-2 on the road this year. For this team to go 7-2 on the road is pretty cool. It's pretty special. The two games we lost (Iowa State and Missouri) ... we could have won either one of them.

"In the national championship year, the best we could do is 5-3. To win away from home like that is a tribute

Sutherland's successful KU career nears finish

By Matt Tait
news@ljworld.com

When Kansas University senior Aishah Sutherland first was recruited by KU coach Bonnie Henrickson as a senior at Perris (Calif.) High, she had to check out a map to make sure she knew where the Sunflower State was located.

Today, as she prepares for the final home game of her four-year college career — 7 tonight vs. Oklahoma State at Allen Fieldhouse — this West Coast native's imprint is all over the Midwestern program.

Though often overshadowed in the box scores and headlines

SENIOR NIGHT

What: Oklahoma State (14-11 overall, 6-10 Big 12) vs. Kansas (18-10, 7-9)

When: 7 p.m. today

Where: Allen Fieldhouse

TV: Metro Sports (Knology cable chan-

Aishah in the news

Sutherland

CONTINUED FROM PAGE 1B

Heading into the final home game of her career, Sutherland ranks second in career blocks (144), third all-time in rebounding (867) and seventh in games played (125).

None of those totals have surprised Henrickson, even if it took her a little longer than normal to offer Sutherland a scholarship.

"I really just felt that if she would buy in and commit to me growing her game, she had the tools to become a really, really special player," Henrickson said. "You don't play in this league and put up those kinds of numbers and not be significant, and certainly she is."

The first time Henrickson actually saw Sutherland play in person, the ultra-athletic forward logged just one minute of action while playing for what Henrickson said was the best AAU team in the country. Because Sutherland's father, Clinton, had played at the University of Cincinnati — and later professionally overseas — she always leaned on her dad to help shape her

KANSAS UNIVERSITY FORWARD AISHAH SUTHERLAND, left, as a freshman in a photo from Jan. 24, 2009, and right, as a senior on Jan. 31, 2012, will

Shereen, my granddaughter
(My Daughter Saudia's Daughter)

My Granddaughter, Shereen
#3 @ UC IRVINE, 2016-2017

My Neice Elisia, My Sister Beatrice, and I at my
Nephew Freeman Jardan's Wedding, 2016

My Nephew Freeman's wedding
(My Sister Beatrice's son)

My Niece, Elisia's wedding
(My Sister Beatrice's Daughter)

Nation of Islam Prayer Book

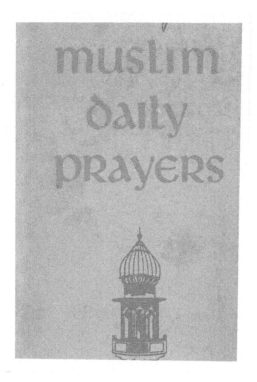

MUSLIM

DAILY PRAYERS

compiled

under the guidance of

Mr. Elijah Muhammad

Messenger of Allah
to the Lost-Found Nation of Islam
in North America

for the use of members
of MUHAMMAD'S
TEMPLES OF ISLAM
throughout the United Sates of America

THE STOKES

My Husband, Ronald Stokes

Postcard from Ronnie

"A Little Deer Sends Greetings from Maine"

P142

As-Salaam-Alaikum:

WORKING hARD! GIVE EVERYbody ThE GREETINGS. I hoPE yOU RECEIVED mY leTTER MY NEPhEW MAiLed it. HOPE to SEE YOU NEXT TUESDAY.

YOUR BROTHER,

R.T.X.

Post Card

ADDRESS

Miss. DELORES JARDAN
5420 So. ELLIS Ave.
Chicago 15, ILLINois

A "LITTLE DEAR" SENDS GREETINGS.

My Wedding to Ronnie

Me at My Wedding With
My Mom and My friend Stephanie

Mr. & Mrs. Stokes, Ronald's Parents

Bea Jones (Ronald's Sister, My Sister-in-law)

Donna, Bea Jones Stokes' Daughter, My Neice

Gregory, Bea's Son, My Nephew

Earnie, Bea's Son, My Nephew

Deron, Bea's son

Deron, Ronald's Nephew and Saudia, My Daughter

Ronald, Br. Randolph, Br. Willie, Circa 1958

Muslims Arrested After Refusing To Send
Their Children to Public School.
My Mother Is The Fourth Person In The Center Top.

OUR-PIONEERS

fought for the Right to
Be muslim, Practice
their Religion and To be
an Educational Institute
of their own.
1935

2118 East Violet Drive
Phoenix 40, Arizona
May 3, 1962

Mrs. Delores Jordan
Mosque No. 27
Los Angeles, California

As-Salaam-Alaikum

In the Holy Name of Almighty Allah, the Beneficent, the Merciful Saviour. To Him alone do I submit and seek refuge.

Dear Sister Delores:

I share with you the grief that the unwanted and unwelcomed visitors left with you and your home last week, April 27, 1962.

May Allah repay the devils with death and a quick one! I will not let them rest until there is revenge for the death of our brother.

As-Salaam-Alaikum

Your brother,

Elijah Muhammad,
Messenger of Allah

EM:bc

Condolence Letter from Hon. Elijah Muhammad
After My Husband Ronnie Was Murdered.

Bilalian News
Historical Black Muslim Newspaper, May 1978

Bilalian News
Historical Black Muslim Newspaper, July 1978

"New World Patriotism Day" in Chicago, Illinois extolls human life and dignity.
Photo by Wali Akbar Muhammad

Imam Wallace Deen Muhammad—A Balanced Muslim pg. 17

BRAINSTORMING: New Careers staff members discussing their academic plans include, from left, Stephanie Roderick, bookkeeper-secretary; Erdine Travis, counselor-intake coordinator; Lori Yamashita, instructor; William Nash, program director; Brenda Russell, instructor, and Delores Jordan, instructor.

Me Before I Started Teaching In Public Schools

Thank You Letter From Student

May 3, 1995

Dear Mrs. Jordan,

How are you?

I was very pleased to hear
that you are still teaching
at Manual so that I
could express my appreciation
and gratitude for having
you as a teacher. I really
enjoyed your accounting
class. I don't know if
I would have chosen accounting
as my career if I had
not taken your class
and enjoyed it.

I just wanted to say thank
you for the inspiration

You made accounting fun, enjoyable
and interesting to me. For that
I care alot since I will
be graduating from Loyola
Marymount University with a
degree in Accounting.

Thanks for everything that
you said and did while
I was in High School that
encouraged me to pursue
my dreams.

Sincerely,
Georgette M. Green

Me and Imam Warith Deen Muhammad,
Elijah Muhammad's Son, Circa 2005

Made in the USA
Las Vegas, NV
10 July 2023

74472724R00142